Rights and Wrongs In The Arab-Israeli Conflict

To the Anatomy of the Forces of Progress and Reaction in the Middle East

This book is an expanded version of an essay under the same title that first appeared as a special, September 1967, issue of The Minority of One, *an independent monthly journal of analysis and opinion.*

Rights and Wrongs In The Arab-Israeli Conflict

To the Anatomy of the Forces of Progress and Reaction in the Middle East

by M. S. Arnoni Introduction by D. F. Fleming

The Minority of One Press
A Division of The Minority of One, Inc.
155 Pennington Avenue, Passaic, N. J. 07055

Library of Congress catalog card number 68-18700
Designed by Martin Stephen Moskof
Printed in the United States of America

101

—to Yoav

Table of Contents

Introduction

D. F. Fleming

This book is important, because it deals honestly with the phenomenon that Israel is now regarded as an aggressive tool of Anglo-American imperialism by the communist countries and most of the Third World.

The author shows clearly that this was not true in 1947, when Israel was winning her independence from Britain and Andrei Gromyko was pleading for her right

---

Dr. D. F. Fleming, Emeritus Professor of International Relations at Vanderbilt University, is the author of the two-volume history of *The Cold War and Its Origins, 1917-1960*, published in New York, London, Milan, Athens and Tokyo, as well as of other works. He has twice been a member of the Institute for Advanced Studies and twice a Fulbright Lecturer overseas.

to live; that the weight of Arab leadership was one on the side of the Germans during World War II; and that since 1945 exiled Nazis have positions in Egypt, facilitating the most fantastic stories of Jewish crimes. He documents irrefutably the will of the Arabs to exterminate the Israelis, describes their plan for doing so in May 1967, and the fate of the remaining Jews in Arab countries when the plan failed.

The book recognizes that Israel's difficulties with most of the non-Western world arose from the decision of the Soviet Union to ally herself with the Arabs, deplores the failure of Israel to work harder to escape from exclusive reliance on the United States, and urges greater efforts in this direction in the future. Ben-Gurion is strongly criticized for subservience to the United States.

Since it is plain that the Middle East has become a tragic victim of the Cold War, Arnoni urges that it be exempted from that struggle, that the Soviet Union cease its arming of the Arabs and the United States its efforts to control the Mediterranean. He pleads for them to join in a great development plan which would absorb the Arab refugees, with Israel's active help, and for a never-ending effort on Israel's part to hold out to the Arab world "a promise of mutually advantageous relations."

Aware throughout of the difficulties of objectivity, the author has contributed insights and information which could lead to an amelioration of the sad situation in the Middle East—if the clashing ambitions of the two great powers, including control of Mid-East oil, will permit.

Palo Alto, Calif. D. F. Fleming

Truth by Alliance

M. S. Arnoni

Reincarnations of Sheiks and Monarchs

The overwhelming support given the Arabs in their struggle against Israel by the Third World and the communist governments effectively projects the image of the Arab countries as progressive forces challenged by a Jewish state that is a creation and tool of Anglo-American imperialism. There are so many paradoxes involved in this presentation that the question arises why they are so commonly overlooked and why judgments are made in spite of them.

The main reason is that many people find substitutes for inquiry and information as a basis of judgment. Either intellectually or impulsively they presume the validity of the substitutes, one of which is the general view of the world as a theater of struggle between old exploitative forces and the newly emerging forces of freedom and progress. Since such a struggle is indeed taking place, involving most of what transpires in international politics, there is the assumption that in the Middle East, too, the acute conflict is primarily, if not exclusively, a part of it.

This being the view of the Middle East even before one actually engages in direct observation, one must necessarily identify in that region those contending forces which are usually at play wherever imperialist ambition encounters challenge. Thus analogies are derived not from reality but from an abstraction. Whereas it is essential for an analogy to be based on the coincidence of the respective situations *from which* and *for which* it is drawn, fallacious analogies limp along on one leg, with information essentially confined to the situation *from which* it is drawn; the applicability to the situation *for which* it is drawn is merely presumed.

By this logic, one is bound to discern in the Middle East a corresponding factor for each that is or was present, let's say, in Vietnam, pre-independent Algeria or racist South Africa. There must be an equivalent to the Diems or Kys, as there must be to the innocent, decimated Vietnamese, the interventionist Americans, the national liberation forces, and all the rest. The only task is to pair off the Vietnamese (or Algerians, Angolans, Cubans, etc.) and their Middle Eastern "counterparts."

This is easy, very easy. The "basic" demarcation line between the presumed forces of national liberation and those of imperialism having been drawn, everything falls into line automatically. One merely needs to take note of which countries support which. Since throughout the world the Americans and/or other imperialist powers maintain systems of tutelage, such support as they give Israel "proves" Israel to be nothing but a counterpart of those systems. Since the Arab governments appear to be on the other side, and since they are supported by those socialist governments which elsewhere support the forces of national liberation and progress, they, the Arab governments, are presumed to be the forces of national liberation and progress in the Middle East.

Even a perfunctory examination proves these assumptions to be folly. Are the Saudi Arabians part of the national liberation forces confronting imperialism-serving Israel, or are they themselves an imperialism-serving force that is being challenged by the UAR in the Yemen? Is Jordan a tool of imperialism, as Nasser and his aides have assured us, or does she deserve the praise of revolutionary councils that stand by her against Israel? Is Hussein a "prostitute," as Nasser has called him, or is he a "great brother," as Nasser has also called him? Is the Ba'ath regime in Syria progressive, socialist and revolutionary, as Nasser (and Soviet leaders) has assured us, or is it a "fascist," "Nazi" and "dictatorial" regime[1], as Nasser has also assured us?

Nasser, the jailer of communists, is praised by communist governments. At times, he is condemned, for cooperating with those governments, by Syria's ruling party, which itself is responsible for outlawing the communists, and which, however, is praised by the communist governments even more. Which praise and which condemnation is justified? Or are they, paradoxically, all justified? Is Iraq part of the national liberation movement by virtue of opposing Israel, or is it a Soviet-condemned tyranny, suppressing and warring on its Kurdish minority? Is it a natural ally of the Soviet Union? Had not its regime seized power from Abd al-Karim in 1963 and executed him for the "sin" of too close relations with socialist countries? Or is Iraq progressive despite being reactionary?

Is the Sudan progressive? Or does it kill its black southern population by the millions? Or is it, perhaps, progressive despite doing so? And what of Kuwait and the other Arabian sheikdoms? Are they suddenly progressive? anti-imperialist? the epitome of peoples struggling for self-determination and dignity? Are they imperialist tools or imperialist challengers? By what revolutionary logic, and by what known colonial relationship, could they conceivably be both, alternating in their contradictory roles? Should we instantly forget

[1] Nasser's statement of August 12, 1963.

things we have been told about certain governments and political movements and equally instantly believe in the opposite?

How to Become an Imperialist Without Really Trying

The presumed imperialist sinfulness of Israel is no less questionable than the anti-imperialist purity of the Arab governments. The first inaccuracy concerns the genesis of the Israeli state. It was *not* established as a creature of British imperialism, but in defiance of it. It emerged as a result of a prolonged campaign of civil disobedience and armed struggle by the Israelis against the British occupants of Palestine. Curiously enough, in challenging the British, President Nasser was an Israeli apprentice of sorts. He mentions in a book that, during a lull in the Palestine fighting in 1948, he tried in conversations with Israeli officers to learn from them methods of anti-British resistance.

When the British, after failing to defeat a prolonged Jewish insurgency, vacated the country, they did so in the hope that the Arabs would accomplish what they themselves had failed to accomplish, and that they would then return to Palestine behind the victorious Arab Legion, which they directly commanded, equipped and financed. It was Major I. C. Clayton, the British Foreign Office's liaison man with the Arab League, who secretly planned and coordinated the invasion of what was to be the Jewish state by the armed forces of Egypt, Transjordan, Iraq and others. Those forces were under the command of such "progressive" people as Egypt's playboy, feudal potentate and king, Farouk; the old messenger of British colonialism in Iraq, Prime Minister Nuri Said Pasha; the British regal invention King Abdullah, and such "private" military inter-Arab leaders as Fawzi el Kawukji, the notorious Nazi collaborator.

Because of these historic facts Israel gained her independence not contrary to the position of the socialist governments but with their full political support and even military aid. The political support was expressed in the 1947 vote of the Soviet Union and the other socialist countries, in the United Nations, for the partition of Palestine; the military assistance came in the form of arms sent the Israelis, with Moscow's blessings, primarily by Czechoslovakia.

Accusations that Israel is nothing but a tool of *American* imperialism are contradicted by clear facts at least as far as the 1956 Sinai campaign is concerned. While at the time acting in collusion with France and Great Britain, Israel clearly displeased the United States, invoked her wrath and was subjected to her severe pressure to vacate the captured Sinai Peninsula. This is a rather peculiar relationship if we are to accept that Israel is merely a United States satellite. Certainly, neither the American hirelings in Saigon nor the ones on Formosa, the Philippines or Puerto Rico can be imagined in an equivalent policy relationship with the United States.

If indeed Israel were a willing tool of Western imperialism, she would not have many of her life-threatening problems. For then she should be able to get along excellently, at least with Faisal of Saudi Arabia and with Hussein of Jordan, whose imperialism-serving status is appreciated universally and is a major reason for inter-Arab quarrels and military confrontations.

If all this does not suffice to rehabilitate Israel, perhaps a testimonial or two from seemingly authoritative ideological quarters will be the answer. With Nasser's progressive bona fides firmly established in Moscow, it, conceivably, need not be counter-revolutionary to accept what he and his propagandists have said on one occasion or another. Here is what his Cairo "Voice of the Arabs" broadcast on June 25, 1955:

> Zionism has taken part in every movement of destruction; the last of these is the movement of communism. A Zionist may be a millionaire, but nevertheless he encourages the spread of communism and at the same time finances it with money and propaganda.

That that statement corresponds with President Nasser's own analysis is clear from an address he delivered at a meeting of the "Liberation Rally" on August 21, 1954:

> I have previously told you that it has been definitely established that the communists in this country are working with Zionism. . . . They work as hirelings for Zionism.[2]

The truth is that the considerable degree of coincidence between Israel's policies and various imperialist

2 *Al Ahram,* Cairo, August 22, 1954.

schemes of Western powers has resulted from Israel's bare self-preservation rather than from a willingness to play a divisive role in her region. The Arab governments do not offer Israel cooperation in return for her disassociation from the Western powers; the Soviet Union does not encourage Israeli hopes that a more balanced Israeli foreign policy would be reciprocated by a friendlier Soviet attitude; both are rigid in their hostility and appear implacable. Under these conditions, what should Israel do? Accept the premise that she has no rights, not even that of existence, rather than seek protection wherever she can find it? Why should Israel prefer extinction over accepting whatever support is forthcoming and from wherever it is coming? Of which other state anywhere in the world has it ever been expected that it would rather perish than accept a questionable helping hand? The Soviet Union, in her hour of peril, quite properly did not hesitate to enter a treaty with Hitler-Germany, if only to postpone an attack on her territory. Why should the somewhat lesser devil of Western imperialism be less acceptible if he alone offers to save one's life? We do not say all this in defense of a regrettable Israeli foreign policy, but to make it understood that least of all does it derive from a free choice among equally possible alternatives.

But the truth is also that much less than total harmony prevails between Israel and any of the imperialist powers. How fragile these relationships are is shown in the radical change that has taken place in France's attitude toward Israel. From complicity in 1956 and a close friendship in the following years it has deteriorated to political apprehension in 1967. As for the United States, and indeed the other Western powers, they never made their aid to any of the Arab countries contingent on peace negotiations with Israel, on the enforcement of Israel's right of passage through the Suez Canal or even on the Gulf of Aqaba remaining open to Israeli shipping. They have even largely submitted to and co-operated with the Arab blacklisting of enterprises doing business with Israel. And they have refused to transfer their embassies from Tel-Aviv to Jerusalem, manifesting their continued adherence to an international status for the Holy City. They have severely pressured Israel into giving up the territorial advantages it had gained in the 1956 Sinai campaign, a concession extracted without adequate guarantees for Israeli rights, a circumstance that was to become crucial in 1967. And before the present issues are even partly resolved, we are bound to witness so much more American pressure on Israel as need hardly be used vis-a-vis satellite regimes.

Indirectly, the Soviet Union bears a heavy share of responsibility for Israel's Western orientation. Nowhere is a switch to a balanced foreign policy and to support of national liberation movements more easily imaginable than in Israel. To begin with, the Israeli Left is a powerful and economically entrenched force. Together with the moderate Left it constitutes a vast and politically sophisticated majority. Had the Soviet Union held out the prospect of better relations between the two countries and had she attempted to serve as a bridge to some of the Arab governments, the Israeli Left would have gotten all it ever needed to effect a significant change. But the Soviet Union has made the Israeli Left sterile, unable to present to the nation a practical alternative. It is a measure of the deep roots of the Israeli Left that in spite of this it manages to retain its amazing strength.

This is by no means to say that Israel itself has done all it could to develop and/or maintain better relations with the Soviet Union and other socialist countries. On the contrary, it appears that the successive governments of David Ben-Gurion have deliberately antagonized the USSR. Eager to qualify not only for U.S. economic aid but also for a friendly U.S. attitude toward private Jewish-American contributions to and investments in Israel, Ben-Gurion and his lieutenants displayed little integrity in resisting State Department recipes for Israeli taste preferences. Privately and publicly applying for a mutual defense arrangement with the United States, only to be rejected time and again, Israel made few political efforts to become a member of the Third World in formation, but it made many and determined efforts to keep, deepen and even put on an exclusive basis her friendship with the United States. Even the circumstances in which, in the early days of Israel's independence, the trickling Jewish immigration from East Europe, including Russia, was prevented from assuming more massive proportions are shrouded in suspicion. Nothing is known that would assuage the conjecture that Israel itself, prompted by ominous U.S. whispers, cooled off toward the prospect and poured icy water on a few receptive East European heads.

More revealing is what appears to have been Israel's deliberate neglect of an oppportunity, in 1955, to develop cordial relations, diplomatic, cultural and economic, with China. Israel's one-time ambassador to Burma and at present chairman of the Knesset's Foreign Policy Committee, David Hacohen, disclosed in his book, *Yoman Burma (Burmese Diary*, Am Oved publ., 1963), details of ignored Chinese encouragement he received both in Rangoon and while heading an invited Israeli delegation to Peking. The implication is clear that Israel's leaders did not dare to start a dialogue with China for fear of angering the Americans. The shortsightedness involved was tragic, potentially fatal. Had Israel accepted those early Chinese overtures, she would have gained a diplomatic channel at the very least precluding the present virtually unanimous hostility of the Second and Third Worlds toward her.

Yet, in considering the integrity of a country's international politics, great importance attaches to its size, strength and potential for self-reliance. It is one thing when a country, more or less capable of taking care of itself, lacks the integrity of charting its own international course, and quite another when this is done by a small nation that can afford fewer risks. There is, for example, a great difference between Great Britain's obedience to the United States and the obedience of a country like the Philippines, for the former could pursue an independent diplomatic course with greater ease and security. In the final analysis, Israel's lack of diplomatic courage stemmed from in themselves understandable fears of being completely crushed. This was bad diplomacy, but a small country's unwise refusal to accept risks is not the same as a voluntary offer to act as a big power's mercenary. In any case, the predominantly leftist orientation of the Israeli society was such that a Soviet policy of encouragement would probably have rendered Ben-Gurion's exclusively pro-American and pro-Western line not only more difficult but outright impossible.

It is no accident that Israel has for all these years been cold-shouldered by the Soviets. For Israel's foreign policy is probably precisely what the Soviet Union wants it to be. It enables the USSR to put herself in the position of champion of the Arab cause. It would not pay for the Soviet Union to trade the enthusiasm of the Arab world for a greater international balance in small Israel's foreign policy. That's why the Soviet Union has consistently abstained from any gesture toward the Israeli Left that might have increased its influence on the country's external orientation.

But even if the accusations of Israel's being a tool of imperialism *were* fully justified, since when is extinction deemed the proper punishment even for that? All other culpable regimes and countries are to be corrected, but Israel, for whatever its real or presumed sins, is to be liquidated? Yet, the use to which is put the support the Arabs receive from the communist governments and the Third World goes way beyond installing a more desirable regime in Tel-Aviv; it is determined by no one but the Arab recipients. And the Arabs define their purpose unmistakably: extermination.

Between Oil Interests and Israel

That the political fate of the Middle East is predetermined by its rich and internationally coveted oil deposits has become so universal a truism that few people stop to ponder about the actual mechanics of this relationship. Since Israel is seen associating with the countries whose companies exploit the Middle East oil and whose power is available to protect these interests, Israel is presumed to be implicated in the imperialist exploitation. It is viewed as a guardian of those companies, which in turn are presumed to be guardians of Israel. A further presumption is that since these companies are inimical to the real interests of the Arab masses, the Arab masses are inimical to them and, for the same reason, also to Israel. While such a view of the situation is quite persuasive by virtue of its inner logic, nothing could be farther from reality. It is convincing fiction, but the very opposite of actually prevailing relationships.

Not that their oil interests are not decisive factors

in the Middle East policies of the great powers. With the region holding more than 60 per cent of the world's known oil deposits and actually providing 27 per cent of the world's oil consumption, there can be no question about the strategic significance of the oil. The picture becomes even more ominously clear when one realizes that oil exploitation provides an unmatched profit bonanza for politically powerful American and other enterprises. They have injected themselves into operations between the oil-producing Middle East countries and the European buyers, holding a virtual monopoly since not only the crude oil but also the refineries and distribution networks are owned, or controlled, by them. Just how profitable the operation is is indicated by the fact that a two-year cycle suffices for the Western oil companies in the Middle East to realize in revenue the equivalent of their total investment of about $5-billion. This does not include income from oil refining and distribution. While the companies point to the high royalties they pay the host governments, an intricate system of tax allowances at home, at least in the case of the American companies, further increases the effective profits from these foreign operations.

To what lengths the United States would go to protect and perpetuate the profit bonanza of its oil companies in the Middle East was tragically manifested in 1953, in the case of Iran. Although American companies had held no concessions in that non-Arab Mideastern country, the nationalization of the Anglo-Iranian Oil

Company by the government of the ardently nationalist Dr. Mohammed Mossadegh was deemed intolerable by the U.S. government. So much so that by 1953 the CIA's chief operative in the Middle East, Kermit "Kim" Roosevelt (a grandson of President Theodore Roosevelt, and a remote cousin of President Franklin D. Roosevelt) had masterminded a coup against the government of Mossadegh, restored the Shah's rule, and installed as premier the veteran Nazi collaborator General Fazollah Zahedi.

This did not exhaust the United States' altruistic help to the nationalized British, French and Dutch oil interests in Iran. Having installed a government of the CIA's choice, the United States, in an exercise of its perpetual search for peace, harmony and goodwill, dispatched two Americans to mediate a reconciliation between those interests and the new Iranian rulers. One of those men was Under Secretary of State Herbert Hoover, Jr., whose position in the Department of State was largely due to his being a spokesman for American oil interests, in the first place. The other disinterested peace-maker was Howard Page, vice-president of Standard Oil of New Jersey. Needless to say, their mission was crowned with complete success. With a new consortium established, what could be more fair than that the peace apostles receive a substantial share in it in token payment for their disinterested services? The old Anglo-Iranian Oil Company, including British, French, Dutch and Iranian interests, was to hold in the new consortium a mere 40 per cent. The rest did not revert to Iran, but was divided among five American companies (Standard Oil of New Jersey, Socony-Vacuum Oil Co., Standard Oil of California, Gulf Oil, and Texas), Royal-Dutch Shell and Compagnie Francaise des Petroles. A full 40 per cent for the Americans was a modest payment if one considers that it was a return not only for the personal services of Messrs. Page and Hoover, but also for the historically more decisive exploits of the CIA.

What this historic chapter teaches us is that the United States would resort to every kind of intervention to deal with any government of an oil-producing country in the Middle East that would eliminate the foreign interests, regardless of whether there was an Israel in the area, and no matter what the latter's policies might be. The idea of there raging a struggle between the oil-producing Arab countries and the governments of the foreign exploitative companies, and of Israel somehow tipping the scales in favor of the imperialists is sheer nonsense. In point of fact, with but brief and few exceptions, the relations between the oil-producing Arab countries and the exploitative foreign companies (and their governments) are excellent. Least of all are those Arab countries in rebellion against their foreign exploiters. The Arab regimes which are, at least at times, uncooperative with the West, those of the United Arab Republic and Syria, are *not* oil-producers of realized international consequence. The major oil producers, Saudi Arabia, Iraq,

Kuwait and the other sheikdoms of the Persian Gulf, have either never, or in the case of Iraq only at brief intervals, been antagonistic toward the West. Yet, their hostility toward Israel is implacable.

How totally subservient the rulers of at least some of the oil-producing Arab countries are to the Western interests is best shown in the offer the leaders of the Persian Gulf sheikdoms have made to Britain after Prime Minister Harold Wilson announced, on January 16, 1968, plans to withdraw British forces from East of Suez by 1971: they volunteered to finance a continued British military presence. While the rulers of such sheikdoms as Abu Dhabi, Dibai, Qatar and Bahrein offered to pay Great Britian for the privilege of being occupied by its soldiers, U.S. Under Secretary of State Eugene V. Rostow announced, in an interview broadcast over the Voice of America, on January 19, 1968, that Kuwait and Saudi Arabia were willing to join Turkey, Iran and Pakistan in an American-sponsored military pact to fill what is called a "power-vacuum" resulting from the British withdrawal.

This servility to British and American imperialism has nothing to do with Israel. It is a purely Arab phenomenon. It is triggered not by Israel's existence but by intra-Arab politics. The very survival of the servile Arab regimes depends on their imperialist aegis. They all feel threatened by internal reformist movements, whether or not inspired by Nasser. But even within the medieval, ultra-reactionary social framework, there are rivalries rampant such as with Kuwait being coveted by Iraq and Abu Dhabi by Saudi Arabia.

Precisely because the foreign oil-exploiting companies are vitally interested in maintaining good relations with their host governments, they have traditionally been inimical toward Israel. Their animosity antedates the emergence of that state and, prior to 1948, was directed toward its preclusion. At the very least, Israel is viewed by these interests as an unnecessary headache complicating their relations with the Arab governments and arousing ardent nationalism that endangers their hold on the Middle East's oil. The strong influence of the oil lobby in the U.S. Department of State has in turn caused that branch of the U.S. government to be particularly unfriendly toward the idea, and then the reality, of Israel. Even when the White House was displaying cautious and qualified support for the Jewish nationalist movement, in the post-World War II years, the State Department kept pursuing its own negative policy. James Forrestal, Truman's powerful Secretary of Defense, and himself a bitter opponent of a Jewish state in Palestine, did not hesitate to identify, in *The Forrestal Diaries*, considerations of Middle East oil as responsible for his and many other U.S. officials' position. Bartley C. Crum, an American member of the 1945-1946 Anglo-American Committee of Inquiry on Palestine, reported, in his *Behind the Silken Curtain*, not only persistent State Department lobbying against the Jewish aspirations in Palestine, but also that "each time a promise was made to American Jewry regarding Palestine, the State Department promptly sent messages to the Arab rulers discounting it and reassuring them, in effect, that regardless of what was promised to the Jews, nothing would be done to change the situation in Palestine." (pp. 36-37.) Crum, who based this accusation on a secret State Department file he had studied, concluded that "This file confirmed the charges of double-dealing that had been hurled at both the United States and Great Britain." *(Ibid.)* Truman himself noted in his *Memoirs* that the U.S. Joint Chiefs of Staff objected, in 1946, to an armed implementation of the Anglo-American Committee's recommendation that 100,000 Jewish survivors of the Nazi holocaust be admitted to Palestine—because "They were primarily concerned about Middle East oil and in long-range terms about the danger that the Arabs, antagonized by Western action in Palestine, would make common cause with Russia." (Vol. II, p. 149.)

Even after the Partition Resolution had been adopted, the oil lobby and the obliging U.S. Department of State continued their efforts to forestall the emergence of Israel. Walter Millis, who edited Forrestal's *Diaries*, reported that, on January 21, 1948, Under Secretary of State Robert A. Lovett showed Forrestal a document of the Planning Staff of the State Department concluding that the partition plan was "not workable." (p. 360.) On January 29, 1948, a meeting took place between Forrestal and high State Department officials, including

Dean Rusk and Loy Henderson. "Henderson took the position that the vote of the General Assembly for partition amounted merely to a recommendation, not a final decision of the United Nations itself, and that American support of the recommendations was predicated upon the assumption that it would prove 'just and workable.' Forrestal asked whether there was not already sufficient evidence 'to support a statement that unworkability of the proposed solution would justify re-examination.' " (*Ibid.*, p. 362.) Forrestal's *Diaries* further report that Secretary of State George C. Marshall himself was considering and recommending to the National Security Council such alternatives to the partition plan as a joint Anglo-American mandate over Palestine, a trusteeship, or a cantonal system as once suggested by the British. Jorge Garcia-Granados, a Guatemalan diplomat whose own government was some day to be deposed by the CIA, and a member of the United Nations Special Committee on Palestine, reminds us, in his *The Birth of Israel*, that "Certain persons in the United States began to play their part, too, in the process of sabotage. In January [1948], American officials in Washington quietly began to suggest that partition was unsound and cited the disorders in Palestine as proof that it should be reversed." (p. 271.) He further recalls that, on February 24, 1948, the chief American delegate to the United Nations, Senator Warren R. Austin, "announced that the Security Council was not empowered to enforce a political decision—in short, could not enforce partition."

The oil lobby's and State Department's opposition to the emergence of Israel lasted until the very moment of that state's birth. On March 19, 1948, Austin announced U.S. abandonment of partition and endorsement of a trusteeship; Secretary Marshall stated that the new proposal had President Truman's approval. According to Garcia-Granados, "In a number of private talks at Lake Success, New York and Washington, representatives of the United States State Department exerted the strongest possible pressure on Jewish leaders in an effort to persuade them not to proclaim a state. Veiled threats of possible American disfavor, even of severe economic sanctions, were expressed. According to my information, at one point Mr. Truman's airplane, the Sacred Cow, was offered to members of the Jewish Agency Executive then in the United States to fly them to Jerusalem, if they would agree to take up with their colleagues there the possible postponement of a proclamation of independence." (*Op. cit.*, pp. 284-285.) All of which caused the Guatemalan diplomat to conclude that "Partition was not voted under pressure of the United States. It was voted because of the tireless efforts of those in the United Nations and in the world who believed in its justice and historic necessity." (p. 269.)

The anti-Israeli bias of the imperialist oil lobby and State Department survived all the phases of the Arab-Israeli conflict, played a particularly important part in the aftermath of the 1956 Egyptian-Israeli war, and continues unabated to this day. As a product of that bias, there operates in the United States the American-Arab Society, with headquarters in Houston, Texas. It is headed by Douglas Marshall, executive vice-president of the Quintana Petroleum Company of Houston, and its members consist of as many as eighty oil companies that are dealing with Arab countries. The Society is planning to build in Houston a Center for Arabic Studies with the cost of the first stage envisaged as between two and three million dollars. *The New York Times* reported, on January 21, 1968, that "Officials of the society . . . will discuss the center with the leaders of nine Arab nations, Mr. el-Din [the secretary-general] said, in an effort to gain financial support, materials and educators." How completely subordinated the Society is to the Arab governments is revealed in the fact that a "friendship mission to the Arab world," which the Society had planned to send on January 28, 1968, "has been postponed after a meeting with Arab ambassadors to the United States." *(Ibid.)*

The episodes here recounted are but a few samples of an unending chain of events, all of which disprove any complicity between Israel and that Western imperialism in the Middle East whose function it is to protect and broaden exploitative oil interests. On the contary, they prove that whether or not this is known to the Arab masses, they share their real enemies with Israel.

In truth, Jewish influence on American Middle East

policies has on occasion been significant, even if we allow for discrepancies between election campaign rhetoric and behind-the-scenes diplomacy. But this does not stem from an amicableness between the Jews and the oil lobby, such amicableness, or even mutual tolerance, hardly being in existence. It stems from the voting strength of the American Jews. Whatever the particulars of that political influence, they have absolutely nothing to do with imperialism, and they have no more to do with the American oil lobby.

Yet, a monumental injustice is being perpetrated on the Arab peoples in their governments' oil dealings with foreign companies. These injustices are twofold: the Arab nations realize a too small share of the revenue generated by their oil; and, even more importantly, the revenue realized does not serve to modernize and improve the lives of the people in a scope and speed commensurate with the earnings involved.

One can, of course, blame imperialism for both aberrations, and in so blaming be perfectly right. Yet, imperialism, too, does not operate in a void. In this case it operates amidst the Arab nations. So far, none of them has proved either imaginative or persistent in resisting imperialism, and most have been outright cooperative and subservient. This goes not only for such Western satellites as Saudi Arabia and Kuwait, but even for Iraq and Syria, the latter of which is generally viewed as under the most radical and anti-imperialist of all the Arab regimes. Instead of an all-out offensive to turn their oil into a real national resource, by fully controlling its production and sale, Arab governments, lacking in technical and administrative self-confidence, are forever willing to bargain away concessions to foreign interests. Quite typically, *The New York Times* of December 11, 1967, reported that "the Iraqi government had asked for about $400-million as cash payment for the granting of a contract to the Compagnie Francaise des Petroles for the right to exploit the North Rumaila field." An agreement signed between Iraq and the Soviet Union on December 24, 1967, proves that the former has no ideological conditions for foreign concerns to which sectors of the national economy are contracted out. The Russians are not only to provide technical assistance and machinery for oil drillings, but also to help market the extracted petroleum. Their payment is to be in crude oil. The Syrians, too, have, at the end of 1967, been reported courting the French in the hope that they would undertake to market their newly discovered oil internationally.

It is hardly decisive which big power it is whose enterprises are given concessions to exploit a small country's natural resources; the only way to assert national independence, not only economically, but also politically and militarily, is for a country to make itself its own boss. Small and physically weak as a country may be, in today's international complexities, opportunities do arise in which a big power cannot afford committing the needed military means to the acquisition or retention of specific economic interests. But, in order for a government to take advantage of such opportunities, it must be idealistically motivated and politically competent. These are the qualities of which there is a tragic dearth in the Arab world. How tragic is shown by the fact that even Nasser considers implacable hostility toward Israel to take precedence over the Arab world's emancipation from bondage to foreign oil interests. Rather than practice coexistence with Israel, he does not mind, in the aftermath of the June 1967 war, accepting subsidies from Saudi Arabia and Kuwait. These subsidies, which in fact represent Western companies' oil royalties, are thus allowed to spread and deepen political dependence in the Middle East—a prospect obviously more acceptable to Nasser than opening the Suez Canal to Israeli shipping.

This is the more irrational because Israel, with her administrative and technical skills, could provide disinterested guidance that might eventually lead to Arab oil truly being Arab property. If Israel can guide a Ghana into becoming a merchant marine power, she may also have both the efficiency and comforting smallness to provide equivalent disinterested services to her immediate neighbors.

Certainly, in the complex of oil interests in the Middle East, Israel is not on the exploitative side. To misconstrue her part as a convenience of the foreign oil interests is to totally misunderstand the region's realities. The reactionary and exploitative part played in the field of the Middle East's oil is wholly Western and Arab but to no degree Israeli.

Soviet "Zionism"

In 1947, when the issue of Palestine was being debated in the United Nations, the Soviet position was determined by considerations quite different from its present ones. Its political end then having been the removal of British colonial domination, the USSR was supporting the Jewish independence struggle. It could then afford to be objective and also to display that human compassion and understanding for the tragedy of the Jews which one would expect of a country that had been overrun by Nazi hordes.

Much of what Soviet spokesmen were saying then applies with equal force today, even if, for reasons of their own, today's Russian diplomats choose to be oblivious to this. It is particularly relevant to recall some of the things which Andrei Gromyko stated on May 14, 1947, before the U.N. General Assembly:

> The Jewish people suffered extreme misery and deprivation during the war. It can be said without exaggeration that the sufferings and miseries of the Jewish people are beyond description. It would be difficult to express by mere dry figures the losses and sacrifices of the Jewish people at the hands of the fascist occupiers. In the territories where the Hitlerites were in control, the Jews suffered almost complete extinction. The total number of the Jews who fell at the hands of the fascist hangmen is something in the neighborhood of six million. . . . It may be asked whether the United Nations, considering the very serious

> situation of hundreds of thousands of Jews who have survived the war, should not show an interest in the situation of these people who have been uprooted from their countries and from their homes. . . . The fact that not a single Western European state has been in a position to guarantee the defense of the elementary rights of the Jewish people or compensate them for the violence they have suffered at the hands of the fascist hangmen explains the aspirations of the Jews for the creation of a state of their own. It would be unjust not to take this into account and to deny the right of the Jewish people to the realization of such an aspiration.

And then Mr. Gromyko addressed himself to the respective historic rights of Arabs and Jews in Palestine:

> We have to bear in mind the incontestable fact that the population of Palestine consists of two peoples, Arabs and Jews. Each of these has its historical roots in Palestine. That country has become the native land of both these peoples, and both of them occupy an important place in the country economically and culturally.

If this sounds to some like "Zionism," they had better be reminded that the speaker was neither Ben-Gurion nor Eshkol, but an official representative of the Soviet Union.

Ironically, Mr. Gromyko's guideline for a solution was compatible with that preached by Zionists; incompatible with that preached by the Arabs. And the same holds true about that guideline even today:

> Neither history nor the conditions which have arisen in Palestine now can justify any unilateral solution of the Palestine problem either in favor of the creation of an independent Arab state, ignoring the lawful rights of the Jewish people, or in favor of the creation of an independent Jewish state, ignoring the lawful rights of the Arab population. . . . A just settlement can be found only if account

is taken in sufficient degree of the lawful interests of both peoples.

What has changed, since the day when these "Zionist" arguments of Mr. Gromyko's were uttered, to make his speeches of today so different in assumptions, tone and impact? What, instead, enables him and his colleagues now to display such utter one-sidedness of concern and to speak of Israel's right of survival in sufficiently meaningless and non-enforceable terms so as to disturb not even the most virulent Arab chauvinist? What enables them to talk of Hitler's victims as his spiritual successors? Has Jewish history suddenly changed? Have the Israelis reversed themselves, now no longer advocating regional coexistence, and have the Arabs reversed themselves, now being the enthusiasts of coexistence, to warrant the Soviet reversal of attitude?

What *has* changed is but one main factor: the objective of Soviet diplomacy in the Middle East. In 1947, it was to weaken the British colonial hold on the Middle East; today, it is to curry favor with the Arab states, such as they are.

And because the objective of Soviet policy has changed, its authors claim full liberty to rewrite history, distort facts and to serve expediency by obliviousness to once cherished affirmations of life, construction and coexistence.

On Trading Countries

Soviet and French leaders have been linking the Middle East and Vietnam conflicts. The Soviet Union has encouraged Arab bellicosity in many ways. One of them was to supply sophisticated arms, precipitating a hazardous and exhausting regional arms race. Another involved a strange diplomatic incident. Israel's Foreign Minister, Abba Eban, related in the U.N. General Assembly that his Prime Minister was confronted, on the night of May 28, 1967, by the Soviet Ambassador with the complaint of heavy troop concentrations on Israel's northern frontier. When the Ambassador was offered at that very moment to visit any part of Israel, he "brusquely refused." The implication is clear that the Soviet Union was not going to risk a desirable fiction by exposing it to verification. It needed this fiction in order, as President Nasser has admitted on June 9, 1967, to alarm the Arabs about an alleged impending Israeli attack against Syria. As tensions were rising in the Middle East, the Soviet Union was displaying amazing calm.

Even after the United Arab Republic evicted the U.N. troops and imposed a blockade on the Gulf of Aqaba, the Soviet U.N. delegate, Dr. Fedorenko, time and again found it "necessary to stress" that the Soviet Union "does not see sufficient grounds for such a hasty convening of the Security Council and the artificially dramatic climate. . . ."

Now, a war later, even the solutions of the Vietnamese and Middle Eastern crises are presented by the USSR and France as being inter-dependent.

All this suggests that the USSR may have wished for a Middle Eastern conflict in order to create pressure for an American let-up in Vietnam. The theory might have been that a Middle Eastern conflict, with its inherent threat of escalating respective big power involvement, would be so unacceptable to a Vietnam-preoccupied United States, as to induce negotiated settlements in both areas.

If this is indeed what has been on the Soviet (and French) leaders' minds, then the scheme involves particularly Machiavellian cynicism that some day might call for all kinds of unfair sacrifices on the part of any small country.

Not that there would be anything wrong with launching two, three or four Vietnams so as to save the Vietnamese from the monopoly of genocidal U.S. fury. It is well nigh possible that the simultaneous armed assertion of oppressed peoples in more than one spot is the last hope for extricating the Vietnamese from the Americans' nation-murder; and it may also be the other peoples' only prospect for launching an effective struggle for freedom. But the condition of each new Vietnam must be that it actually be a Vietnam. Only if oppression and foreign exploitation do prevail in a country, is a struggle of and for its people justified. It is the identity of interests and moral implications involving two or more countries that provides the sole justification for a coordinated struggle. To involve one country or another in crisis, danger or war for reasons utterly extraneous to it is preposterous. Let us assume that the exposure to danger of Sweden, Albania, East Germany or Kenya could somehow produce a diplomatic situation conducive to negotiating a Vietnamese *modus vivendi.* Would such exposure be permissible? Should, let's say, the Soviet Union or France "volunteer" *them* as an expedient of achieving a desirable end elsewhere?

By the same token, if the United Arab Republic was encouraged in its aggressiveness *vis-a-vis* Israel in the hope that this would produce needed deflection of U.S. military preoccupation from Vietnam, a most reckless international justification of means by ends has been provided.

Some people have gone so far as to criticize the Soviet Union for not intervening militarily to prevent the defeat of the Arabs by Israel. They believe the Soviet leaders to have displayed in the Middle East the same type of appeasement as they are displaying in Vietnam. There is the apprehension that a general Soviet principle has been confirmed of letting aggressors have their own way rather than assuming any risks for the USSR itself.

The thinking behind this criticism, too, is based on a false analogy. While it is true that the Soviet Union has been displaying little determination in coming to the aid of Vietnam, it is also true, as we have already argued, that Israel is not Vietnam. Whether a display of determination is commendable or not must, obviously, depend on whether or not the particular end is worthwhile for which it is employed. It is possible that Soviet softness in the 1967 conflagration in the Middle East is of the same kind as Soviet softness on Vietnam, but that does not mean that in both cases a worthwhile cause is being betrayed. Yet, some people in the socialist and anti-imperialist camp would have welcomed direct Soviet intervention in the Middle East not so much because they think the Arabs deserving of it as to have Soviet willingness to come to the aid of its allies generally confirmed. To us it seems, however, that the fate of any nation is too important a matter to be merely considered a sort of testing ground. The Middle East should be treated with such integrity as precludes its use for an important but irrelevant rehearsal.

While one is on sound moral grounds when petitioning the Soviet Union for whatever exertion is needed to effectively save the innocent, valiant and victimized Vietnamese people, to petition for equally unlimited aid for governments which propose to wipe out another country is least of all of the same moral quality. The only valid analogy between Vietnam and Israel is in the fact that both are the targets of extermination policy, the former by the Americans, the latter by the Arabs. Aid in the defense of a people against its exterminators is the opposite of aid to would-be exterminators of a people.

It is the mentality of the American militarists which usually finds the justice of a particular American position to be less important than displays of toughness for their own sake. According to them, any U.S. position, right or wrong, must be upheld in order that the whole world be taught "respect" for U.S. dictates. Those who offer an alternative to that bandit philosophy may never embrace the "principle" that, in international affairs, toughness for its own sake is more important than justice.

If anything, the vehemence with which the Soviet Union has been castigating Israel and championing the cause of the Arab states suggests that the USSR uses the Middle East conflict to deflect criticism of the weakness of its position on Vietnam. The distrust of the Soviet Union for not providing effective deterrence against the decimators of the Vietnamese people, a distrust that keeps spreading throughout the world of rising expectations, has caused its leaders to try to make up with invective against Israel for that which it refuses to undertake in behalf of Vietnam.

This hardly takes courage, or principle. Encouraging intransigent Arabs into exposing themselves to Israeli punishment is no heroism, and invective thrown at a threatened Israel is a poor substitute for such risk-taking as alone might stop the American genocide of the Vietnamese.

While disunity is shattering the socialist world and centrifugal forces are at play in Moscow, Peking, Havana, the jungles of Latin America and elsewhere, the Soviet leaders seem to settle for an *Ersatz* unity such as demagoguery has produced on the issue of the Middle East. Such verbal patches cannot hide the wound of despair inflicted by the realization of a growing number of peoples that they have in the Soviet Union no protector against imperialists. If the Soviet Union wants to demonstrate that this is not so, that it does stand by its allies and friends, that it does not acquiesce in U.S. expansionism, the place to demonstrate this is Vietnam, not the conference rooms of the United Nations.

Ideological Consistency and Facts

Some people may find specific background information irrelevant to the "real" issues at stake in the Middle East. They might consider it minutiae that merely obfuscate a clear picture of the situation. They would insist on the "over-all" view, in which nothing may be allowed to block the clear demarcation between the imperialist and anti-imperialist forces. With this approach, what is true about a specific situation does not merely depend on the situation but on some overriding, all-embracing abstract. But this is patently folly. For in it the general scheme of things does not consist of integral components such as they are, but possesses, irrationally, retroactive powers of creation. Abstracts are no longer reflections of reality, but its gods, creators and remolders. It is like statistics that are not based on count, but, arbitrarily determined, are forcing life into compliance. Wrongs are no longer necessarily wrongs, and rights are no longer necessarily rights. You can be wrong even if you are right, and you can be right even if you are wrong. How you are depends no longer on what you are, but on the way the consistency of an abstraction—ideological, political, artistic or other—requires you to appear.

This is a consistency of theoretical configuration, it is a grammar embraced with such theoretical intoxication as to make one forget the language it is supposed to serve. What results is a sovereignty of words, charts and symbols. Whatever happens in real life, to living people, can have no bearing on the theoretical equations. A whole world may go down in ruin, or merely be confined, let's say, to Siberian labor camps, but the chalk on the blackboard proves, and proves conclusively, that this is paradise. Or, you can have a political entity volunteer genocidal profession of intent, yet somehow this may be figured out to be irrelevant, or the opposite of what it is.

Perhaps letters I received from two of my radical colleagues indicate the depth of the moral dilemma involved. One of them said in conclusion: "I am sorry that you do not understand that there are some things that are more important than Jews." Before anyone might draw an erroneous conclusion, let me quickly vouch for that man's not being anti-Semitic *per se*. The other correspondent was more elaborate: "I have little use for morality. I would sanction and probably commit every crime in every legal code and decalogue in the world to end war or the rule of the rich. I admire Lenin and Machiavelli. Albert Schweitzer disgusts me. I am interested in facts and the defeat of our enemies.

Everything else is a matter of ethics and good manners."

As this man came close to saying himself, here is ideology replacing ethics. And if ideology is replacing ethics, then any act that subordinates life to ideology is ethical. Hence that "there are some things that are more important than Jews." And if you ask President Johnson, there are "some things that are more important than Vietnamese." And if you ask the Greek fascists, then there are "some things that are more important than the Turkish Cypriotes," while to the "progressive" Arabs not only are there "some things that are more important than Jews," but also more important than their own Yemeni brothers who may therefore be gassed with impunity, and also more important than the Negro Sudanese, who may therefore be wiped out by the millions.

One conclusion that necessarily follows from this is that Hitler was wrong merely bibliographically. I mean to say that he read, or wrote, the wrong book. If he had read, or written, the right book, then even if he acted precisely as he did, he would have been right. It is not what you do that is decisive, but the words you think of while doing it. Here we are at the base of an Existential Mysticism, which—I take the pain to say—provides a philosophical bridge between Nazism and any other ideology that claims absolute paramountcy. For Nazism too derived from the vision of the world as a void which can be filled by the sheer dynamics of action. If you are stubborn and aggressive enough, then your premise will prevail, and by virtue of having prevailed, if by no other virtue, it will become a basic truth. The Nazis did not truly believe in any of their premises as absolutes, and they were quite conscious of the manipulation to which they submitted what they called their "sciences." But they did believe that they could establish existential "absolutes," or capricious ones, or self-serving ones.

Well—I tremble to say it, but I must—we do seem to have a leftist equivalent of all that. There is the magic power of willfulness to alter the essence of things, to read some facts out of existence and to read others into existence, and there is the same willingness to pay any price at all in the process. This contradicts historical materialism, but the hiatus is bridged temperamentally. One consults theory only when the inner mechanism of leftist impulses gets stuck or when the voltage of the impulse is weak enough to permit communication with theory. To most alcoholics it matters little on what particular drink they get intoxicated so long as they achieve the state of intoxication. And the warped, temperamental rather than social, leftist may well reach ecstasy not so much from the embraced ideal as from the self-conviction that much, indeed everything, needs to be sacrificed for it. Fanatical dedication to an ideal is quite likely to go hand in hand with a superficial understanding of it. The best believer is the one who understands least. In this frame of mind, it becomes a crazy notion that the Jews are of great importance; no, they are not, ideology is! And the same goes for every people, culture and what not. These existential mystics would hesitate to sacrifice the Arabs no more than they hesitate to sacrifice the Jews.

What these people have lost sight of is that any progressive ideology is merely a grammar of humanism. Even Marx had least of all a mechanistic approach to ideology. He wanted to accelerate certain historic processes not because they were inevitable but because he found them just and desirable. When people forget this, when their ideology, instead of serving as a grammar of humanism, becomes their new monarch, when it can be right irrespective of what it does to human beings, and when any number of people must be sacrificed on the gamble of someone's particular understanding of a particular ideology, then whatever you may call such ideology, I see little difference between its practitioner and the existential mystics in the brown or black shirts.

Morality is not a matter of expertise, but one of values. That's why everyone is quite qualified to be a practitioner. But ideology is a matter of expertise, very much so. In the case of Marxists and other progressives, it involves a tremendous body of knowledge in multiple disciplines. Just think in how many fields the Marxist scholars were not only experts but also pioneers. That's why, unlike with morality, ideology does involve a hierarchy of specialists. Hence that once you accept the paramountcy of ideology, you are also likely to accept an intellectual elite of ideologues. What emerges in real life is an esoteric centrifugence emanating from revered academies in Moscow, Peking, or elsewhere. Now we are confronted by a paradoxical perversion of intent. We had started out on a supra-personal ideological journey that was to take us "above it all" into a precisely figured out and definitely desirable future, and we wound up depositing our trust and reliance in particular organizations and men. And men, or groups of men known as organizations, are errable, capricious, and self-serving. Our journey into the objective has ended at the station of the purely subjective.

And because men are errable, capricious and self-serving, even if they reside in Moscow, Peking, or elsewhere, and even if they occupy the highest positions in state or party hierarchies, it ultimately turns out that the subliminal trust we vested in them to provide us with clues about what is ideologically right in one situation or another, has tied us to the rationalized interest, convenience or expediency of the standard-setting man or institution. More clearly, it is a delusion to think that one's loyalty to particular centers of power is ideological; what really emerges is ill-understood and self-deceptive support of one country's or another country's selfish interests. The real relationship between these interests and the ideological rationalization is no different than in the case of a Johnson assuring us that all he is interested in is "freedom and democracy" or "peace with justice."

I am not talking about anyone's being a slave to anyone else. I am not implying some conspiratorial fifth-column relationship, but I am speaking of such exaggerated enthusiasm one may have for a particular power center as creates, subtly and imperceptibly, an intellectual and moral dependency that can be easily misused. In its ultimate degree, it is not completely unlike the I-only-obey-orders attitude that Eichmann has made so famous.

It is by such mystical powers that a country like Jordan can, despite itself, be accepted as a genuine people's force. It is by such black magic that Saudi slave traders, Kuwaiti sheiks amassing imperialist oil royalties, and Egyptian Nazi collaborators from World War II can be accepted as proponents of progress, socialism and national liberation.

One thing many of the people relying on these criteria fail to appreciate is that they themselves, and the peoples and movements they represent, stand to lose the most from an artificial ideological consistency that frustrates the sanity of one's perception of reality. For their approach spurs on a polarization of international concerns that can only serve one big power or another, in utter disregard of the interests of smaller nations. Essentially, it leaves but two or three observation towers from which events everywhere are to be seen and measured. One figurative observation tower is located in Moscow, another in Peking, and a third in Washington.

If anything happening anywhere must necessarily and exclusively be seen in the context of the imperialist and anti-imperialist confrontation, then each of the contending camps must have an indisputable leader. That leader is the USSR, China or the USA. The leadership need not always be direct, subordination often being enforceable not by physical means but by adherence to common intellectual and political criteria. It is achievable if the prospective subordinates accept *a priori* that their positions on issues of significance must be compatible with that general philosophy of international relations which prevails in their particular choice from among the three ideological world capitals. The danger that arises from this is that the legitimacy of the interests of a particular country no longer depends on their innate merits, but on an extraneous context abstractly superimposed in Moscow, Peking or Washington.

Most clearly we see the application of such a consistency-of-abstracts in Vietnam. Most proponents of the U.S. war do not hesitate to concede numerous ugly and illegitimate aspects of the U.S. intervention and of the Saigon power structure that is upheld by that intervention. They may even concede, as former President Eisenhower has done, that the vast majority of the Vietnamese opt for the political relations the U.S. forces are fighting to prevent. But they point to "overriding" considerations which subordinate and nullify all local merit. "Global considerations" are somehow supposed to reverse what is right and wrong.

If among the socialist and newly independent nations,

too, the adjudication of each local or regional situation should be done in one central computer—whether located in Moscow or Peking—then an international politics would emerge in which everything is subordinated to the rationalized conveniences of but one, two or three big powers. All international decisions would then be left to them, individually or collectively, harmoniously or through contest.

True, there would be nothing new in such a constellation of international relations, but that is precisely why a change is needed. What has been more typical of the colonial era than the predominance of countries whose power sufficed to make their capitals not only their own, but, essentially, also the capitals of other nations? If the post-colonialist era, too, is to be based on that principle, then the identity of usurper rulers of the world may change but not the institution, nor the humiliations and injustices involved. It would be particularly ironic if the small countries themselves, instead of insisting on a balance of sovereignties, upheld its replacement by big power arbitrariness.

To ignore any legitimate interest of Israel in its dispute with the Arabs, on the theory that irrespective of merit the regional situation must be subordinated to a more general good, is to resort to the same ideological, political, intellectual, moral and procedural criteria which the Americans are so consciencelessly applying to Vietnam. But the Vietnamese people are right in their struggle, not because of needed consistency in categorizing world events and trends, nor because of anything going on any place other than their own country, but merely because *they*, in their own country, and in the context of their own problems, are right. Who on the outside is incidentally comforted by the prevalence of their rights is secondary and neither establishes nor annuls these rights. By the same token, who might or might not benefit from the prevalence of legitimate Israeli interests, and whose world view might be served as a result, cannot alter the primary merits of the situation. The contention that it can is like literary critique undertaken not to assess works but to recreate them. It is like sending back those newly born of whom someone disapproves. It reverses the relationship and chronology of cause and effect, origin and consequence, essence and incidence.

No ideological theory is more fallacious than one which depends on a wishful projection of facts instead of being borne out by an independently realistic discernment of them. Ideological consistency is least of all achieved when we close our eyes and say that things are as they are not; its test occurs in the laboratory of life, not in imagination's self-confirmation.

From the History of Arab Nationalism

M. S. Arnoni

The Greatest Arab Hero

The ideological qualities of Arab nationalism have no bearing on the Arab peoples' right to self-determination and all this implies. Whether a preponderance of Arab leaders had during World War II written a creditable or compromising historic chapter in no way alters the fact that the Arab world has for all too long been subjected to imperialist exploitation. Nor does it bestow legitimacy on the continued Western exploitation, intrigue and intervention that stand in the way of the Arab peoples.

But the ideological properties of Arab nationalism are by all means relevant to a discussion of the Arab-

Israeli conflict. Since they provide the frame of reference in which Arab postulates *vis-a-vis* Israel are formed, one must acquaint oneself with those ideological properties if only in order to be able to interpret correctly Arab aspirations.

The relevance of the political quality of Arab nationalism to the present international dispute was underlined by the Syrian President, Dr. Nureddin el-Attassi, when, in the process of addressing the emergency session of the U.N. General Assembly on June 20, 1967, he found it profitable to state:

> the Arabs fought both World Wars and contributed to the liberation of Europe from Nazism and the realization of Allied victory.

Relevant as is this general subject, Dr. el-Attassi did not let historic fact inhibit his imagination. Otherwise he might have recalled that his own kinsman and a predecessor in the Syrian presidency, Hashim el-Attassi, not only congratulated the pro-Nazi rebels in Baghdad in 1941, but also called on all Syrians to help the revolt prevail. (Which, incidentally, did not disqualify him from another, post-war, term as President of Syria.) He might also have reminded us that Syria as well as Egypt, Saudi Arabia and Lebanon did not declare war on Nazi Germany until February 1945, when her defeat had practically been accomplished. They acted only days before March 1, 1945, which was the deadline for the status of belligerent against the Axis—required for membership in the United Nations and participation in its founding conference in San Francisco. (Just the same, the gesture was to be paid for with the life of the Egyptian responsible for it, Prime Minister Ahmed Maher, who was assassinated by the Moslem Brotherhood.)

But the Arab record *vis-a-vis* the Nazis was not merely one of passivity. On the contrary, throughout the Arab world hopes had been placed on Hitler, not only because he was an enemy of the British enemy, but also because the ideology and temperament of Nazism were in many ways attractive to the Arabs. Already in the 1930's John Gunther found that "Hitler is tremendously popular with the Arabs. . . . The greatest contemporary Arab hero is—Adolf Hitler."[3]

In a work outstanding for its scholarship and based on documentation drawn from official German and Arab sources, Lukasz Hirszowicz writes:

> The Arab leaders did not conceal their antipathy to France, their distrust of England and their preference for Germany, even in conversations with the Consul-General of the United States. They did not regard the war in Europe as a misfortune; they pinned their hopes on its weakening the Western Powers. . . . True, certain public figures in Syria, and particularly in Lebanon, held a different point of view, but they were rather isolated in Muslim circles.[4]

For Arabs to be attracted to the Nazis and their ideas was strange indeed: the Nazis had nothing but contempt

---

[3] *Inside Asia* by John Gunther, Harper & Bros., New York, 28th edition, 1939, p. 528.

[4] *The Third Reich and the Arab East* by Lukasz Hirszowicz, University of Toronto Press, 1966, p. 184.

for them. Their "scientists" rated the Arabs racially inferior even to the Jews. In addition, Alfred Rosenberg, the chief Nazi ideologue who was one day to be executed in Nuremberg as a major war criminal, in his book, *The Myth of the 20th Century*, specifically praised British imperialism as a guardian of the white race, and he urged that it remain in India and the Suez so that the onslaught of the "inferior races" against Europe be held back. Only the Arabs' persistent offers of collaboration eventually made the Nazis realize their potential value as fifth columns. The racist contempt for the Arabs was then conveniently overlooked by both sides.

Robert St. John, the renowned correspondent, author and biographer, wrote a sympathetic biography of President Gamal Abdel Nasser after numerous conversations with him and his intimate friends. In it he throws light not only on Nasser's personal attitude toward the Nazis but also on the Egyptian attitude generally:

> The pro-Axis sympathies of most Egyptians at this time were not based alone on the conviction that the Germans and Italians were going to win the war. Nor alone on the Arab proverb: "He who is the enemy of my enemy is my friend." The ideology of the two totalitarian powers was ready-made for a country like Egypt. It reassured the wealthy pashas and beys who were amassing fortunes out of the war and wanted to keep their money. But at the same time the mumbo jumbo of the "socialism" they dispensed fascinated the masses of the poor, the ignorant, and those easily taken in by slogans. There was something in it for every Egyptian. Military men such as young Lieutenant Nasser were impressed by the might of the Wehrmacht and the Luftwaffe, by the military

> genius that had so quickly brought about the fall of Warsaw, Copenhagen, Oslo, Brussels, Paris, Athens, Belgrade.[5]

Nasser himself has confirmed his biographer's impression of his sentiments. In an interview he granted to and had published on the front-page of the notorious neo-Nazi German weekly *Deutsche National Zeitung und Soldaten Zeitung*, on May 1, 1964, the UAR President was quoted as saying:

> During the Second World War our sympathies were with the Germans.

The mobs in the streets of Cairo were jubilantly shouting, "Rommel! Rommel! Rommel."[6] In Nablus, Palestine, crowds were receiving British troops with shouts of "Heil Hitler!"[7] In the streets of Damascus, Homs, Aleppo, a song was heard:

> *Bala Missou, bala Mister*
> *Bissama Allah, oria alard Hitler.*
> (No more Monsieur, no more Mister
> In heaven Allah, on earth Hitler.)[8]

Nasser and the Axis

But the Arabs served Nazi Germany not only with ballads and Hitler salutes. In Arab country after Arab

---

5 *The Boss* by Robert St. John, McGraw-Hill, New York, 1960, p. 40.

6 *Ibid.*, p. 46.

7 Quoted from the French weekly *Marianne* in *The Mufti and the Fuehrer* by Joseph B. Schechtman, Thomas Yoseloff, London, 1965, p. 83.

8 Quoted by Schechtman, *op. cit.*, p. 84, from *The Fighting French* by Raoul, Aglion, New York, 1943, p. 217.

country power plays were taking place in attempts to align them with Germany and/or Italy. Ironically, in Vichy-governed Syria and Lebanon, the Arabs were inclined to help the Nazis beyond anything the Nazis themselves were willing to accept. The Germans, in an attempt not to antagonize their French allies, were leaning over backward in discouraging Arab hopes to be "liberated" by them.

In Iraq, a pro-Nazi revolt led by the regime of Rashid Ali el Kailani broke out in April 1941, and war on Britain was declared on May 2 of that year. Participating in the Iraqi revolt were many Arab leaders who had sought exile in Baghdad after years of rebellion in Palestine. Among them were such eminent personalities as the ex-Mufti of Jerusalem, Haj Amin el Husseini, Fawzi el Kawukji, and Jamal el Husseini.

With the defeat of the Iraqi revolt by the British, most of the Palestine leaders who had participated in it fled to Syria. There, with the help of German agents and the consent of the French Vichy authorities, they organized Arab fighting units.

In Egypt, the government was in the hands of Aly Maher, generally known as "Hitler's man." General Aziz el Masri, earlier deposed for his Nazi sympathies and links, was again to be appointed as the Chief of Staff. So threatened did the British believe their war effort to be that on February 4, 1942, they stormed the Abdin Palace with tanks, confronting King Farouk with an ultimatum to appoint a non-Nazi government or to be deposed. Aly Maher had to go. Ten years later, in 1952, however, as soon as Nasser's military coup proved successful, "Hitler's man" was again to make Egyptian history: he was the first post-revolutionary Prime Minister.

But back in 1942, Nasser and other young officers of the Egyptian army were so disappointed by the removal of the pro-Nazi Prime Minister and Chief of Staff that they resolved some day to take the country's destiny into their own hands. Wrote Nasser to a friend:

> I am ashamed that our army has not reacted against this attack and that she has accepted it, but I am glad that our officers, who until now think only of amusing themselves, at last begin to speak of revenge.[9]

Out of outrage at the failure of attempts to align Egypt with Nazi Germany Nasser and many of his army colleagues established the secret Free Officer organization which was eventually to remove Farouk and to take over the reins of power.

Actually, their pro-Nazi activities had begun long before the British ultimatum. Already in 1941, Nasser and his friends tried to help General el Masri to fly behind the German lines. The General was supposed to be picked up by a German plane bearing R.A.F. markings, but a broken-down automobile made him late for the crucial rendezvous. An alternate plan was put in motion: two of Nasser's friends were to pilot an Egyptian military plane that would take the General to the Germans. One of the pilots was Hussein Zulficar

---

[9] St. John, *op cit.*, p. 45.

Sabry, who was one day to become Nasser's Deputy Foreign Minister, and whose brother, Aly Sabry, is at present Deputy Premier.

El Masri did not make it to the Germans. A take-off accident led to his and the two pilots' arrest. Thereupon Nasser's closest friend, Anwar el Sadat, who was one day to become the Secretary General of the National Union, Minister of State and an otherwise powerful figure in the Nasser regime, sent this message to the unlucky pro-Nazi general:

> Except for ill luck we would have joined forces with the Axis, struck a quick blow at the British, and perhaps have helped win the war. Better luck next time![10]

Attempts to help the former Egyptian Chief of Staff reach the German lines were not the only of Sadat's exploits which Nasser was to reward immediately as well as after he became Egypt's dictator.

> One hot evening that same summer [of 1942] two young officers in British uniform arrived by military car at Sadat's home. The spokesman introduced himself in perfect Arabic as Hussein Gaafer. He told his story cautiously at first. His real name was Herr Appler and he had been born in Egypt of a German mother and an Egyptian father. His companion was Herr Sandy. They were Nazi agents sent by Rommel to establish an intelligence center in Cairo. They had crossed the dessert in a jeep with British markings. Strapped around their waists was almost a quarter of a million dollars in counterfeit British bank notes, manufactured by the Germans. They also had a powerful radio transmitter in the car. Sadat introduced them to [the pro-Nazi officer of the Egyptian Air Force, also a friend of Nasser, Abdul Moneim Abdul] Raouf,

---

10 *Ibid.*, p. 44.

and tried to help them with their espionage problem.[11]

The plot was eventually uncovered and after a personal investigation by Churchill, Sadat's part in it came to light. As an officer, he was court-martialed and sent to a prison camp. But whatever Nasser could do for him suffered no delay:

> one of the first assessments Nasser collected from the members [of the Free Officers' organization] went to pay Sadat's family the equivalent of fifty dollars a month during the entire two years he was in prison.[12]

As for General Masri, as soon as the would-be Nazi *Gauleiter* of Egypt was released from prison in 1945, Nasser sought him out making him his friend and mentor.

The Mufti and His Friends

No one more faithfully epitomizes the vicissitudes of Arab nationalism than the ex-Mufti of Jerusalem, Haj Amin el Husseini. He was head of the Arab Higher Committee comprising the six Arab parties of Palestine, but his prestige in the Arab world and the scope of his political and para-military activities was much broader. Few were the upheavals anywhere in the Arab world in which he didn't play a significant role. On his orders people were killed not only in Palestine but also in Transjordan, Syria, Lebanon, Iraq and Egypt. A map

---

[11] *Ibid.*, p. 47. Accounts about the two German spies and about the attempts to fly General el Masri behind Rommel's lines are included in Sadat's own book, *Revolt on the Nile* (published with an Introduction by President Nasser, Allan Wingate, London, 1957).

[12] *Ibid.*

of his headquarters at various stages of his career would cover not only the entire Middle East, but also Berlin, Rome, Zurich, Paris and many other places. For Haj Amin el Husseini has for decades been the most outstanding personality of Arab nationalism.

Even today, compromised as he is in the eyes of the world due to his notorious war crimes, to most Arab nationalists he continues to be the preeminent leader and source of inspiration. Other leaders, even in official capacities, seek his advice and guidance.

With the collapse of the Iraqi revolt, the Mufti took refuge in the Japanese embassy in Teheran. From there he went to Rome, where he conferred with Mussolini and Ciano. When, in November 1941, he arrived in Berlin, the Germans put at his disposal a headquarters ("Buero des Grossmufti"), from which he coordinated propaganda, espionage and military recruitment that branched out to Yugoslavia, the Nazi-occupied parts of the USSR, the Middle East, Japan, Greece, Africa, India, Indonesia and Java. Wherever the Germans were interested in arousing Moslems, their transmitters beamed the Mufti's messages. He conferred with Hitler and Ribbentrop on the over-all aspects of Nazi Arab policy. He conferred with Himmler, Eichmann and others, urging them to speed up the Final Solution for the Jews.

El Husseini was particularly active in recruiting Moslem volunteers for Nazi units, especially those of the SS. There is tragic irony in the personal friendship and political cooperation between Gamal Abdel Nasser and the one-time leader of Yugoslavia's gallant partisans, President Tito, for another of Nasser's friends and mentors is Haj Amin el Husseini, the war criminal who had done so much to decimate Tito's partisans. Indeed, it appears that no one but the Mufti could have held together the dreaded "Handshar" SS division, which, consisting of Moslem volunteers, specialized in committing unspeakable atrocities on Tito's comrades.

> Despite their elaborate uniforms and the spiritual ministrations of the pro-Nazi Grand Mufti of Jerusalem, Haj Amin el Husseini, the Moslems never seem to have repaid the attention lavished on them. They mutinied while in training in France, and discipline was restored only after the personal intervention of the Grand Mufti. Late in 1943, "Handshar" was returned to the area from which it had been recruited. For a few months the division skirmished with Tito's partisans, and in the process distinguished itself largely by the number of atrocities it committed. The two standard accounts of the Waffen SS state that the Moslems were later transferred to the Hungarian front, where they supposedly fought bravely against the Red Army. . . ."[13]

With this as background, it is perhaps relevant to document the reality of the friendship triangle that adds the ex-Mufti to the Tito-Nasser fellowship. Nasser himself is the source:

> I remember that just after the announcement of the decision to partition Palestine in September 1947, the Free Officers held a meeting and decided to help in the resistance. Next day I knocked on the door of Haj Amin al

---

[13] *The Waffen SS, Hitler's Elite Guard at War, 1939-1945* by George H. Stein, Cornell University Press, 1966, pp. 182-183.

Husseini, Mufti of Palestine, who was then living in Zaitoun. I said to him, "You have need of officers to lead in the struggle and to train volunteers. In the Egyptian Army there is a large number of officers who wish to offer their services. They are at your command any time you wish."[14]

Luckily, Nasser put himself at the Mufti's disposal only after World War II, for otherwise he might have been sent to hunt for one Josip Broz . . . As for the Soviet leaders, at least they cannot be accused of vengefulness; neither the Mufti's anti-Soviet broadcasts from Berlin nor his recruitment of Moslem traitors in Nazi-occupied parts of the USSR obstructs their friendship for Husseini's disciple Nasser. Nonetheless, perhaps it is timely to remind Nasser's Soviet friends:

Particularly intense was the sustained effort to establish and consolidate pro-Axis military units from among the thirty million Moslems in the Soviet Union. The Mufti's anti-Soviet broadcasts were both numerous and fully attuned to the German line. He was in close contact with several Moslem quislings, such as Ali Khan of the Northern Caucasus; Major Dudanginski, head of the Azerbaijan Legion; Dr. Szymkiewicz, Mufti at the German-occupied *Oastland* area (Poland and occupied regions of USSR); Mohammed al Gazani, Moslem poet and one of the leaders of the anti-Soviet Moslem Union; as well as with the Turkestan National Union Committee. It was largely due to Haj Amin's propaganda that on the arrival of the German armies in the northern Caucasus in 1942, five indigene tribes— the Chechens, the Ingushes, the Balkars, the Karachais, and the Kabardines—welcomed them with bread and salt. On August 30, 1942, the Mufti's represen-

---

14 *Egypt's Liberation, The Philosophy of the Revolution* by Gamal Abdul Nasser, Public Affairs Press, Washington, p. 91.

> tative, Said Hamil, was appointed liaison officer between the German Army and Moslem tribes in the Soviet Caucasus. A Moslem priest was sent by the Mufti to accompany five German agents in a parachute jump behind the Soviet lines southeast of Grozny for a sabotage operation known in code as "Mohammed." In the wake of the German retreat in the winter of 1942-1943, large segments of the five tribes, fearing the vengeance of the returning Soviet armies had, together with their women and children, followed the retreating German Army until they reached temporary refuge in large camps in Crimea and along the lower Dnieper. Many of the able-bodied men among them enrolled in General Vlasov's army, while others were formed into special military units and were utilized against the Soviet partisans.[15]

If diplomatic expediency can cause the Soviets to forfeit their own pride and to advertise as "progressive" the associates of their own quislings, perhaps the Israelis need not be all too hurt when Russian leaders equate them with the Nazis . . .

Where Nazism Remains Uncompromised

Least of all was Haj Amin el Husseini lonely in his Berlin self-exile. He had transferred to the Nazi capital not only his headquarters but also many of his old-time associates and lieutenants. In their midst was Rashid Ali el Kailani, the defeated pro-Nazi Premier of Iraq. Others included Wasef Kamal, for many years the Mufti's ally in Palestine, also a participant in the Iraqi rebellion, and now an agent of the German Secret Service; and Fawzi el Kawukji, guerrilla leader in

15 Schechtman, *op. cit.*, pp. 140-141, based on dispatches in the *New York Post*, June 10, 1946; *The New York Times*, August 18, 1946; *Transocean*, June 10, 1943; and *Dagposten*, Stockholm, June 11, 1943.

Palestine, Syria and Iraq. There were many, many others who followed the Mufti into the Axis lands, eager to make a contribution to a Nazi war victory. After the war, virtually all of these Nazi collaborators returned to the Middle East and resumed their local positions of leadership.

Typically, when, in 1947, a delegation of Palestine's Arab Higher Committee was designated to speak before the United Nations, three of its members—Emil Ghouri, Wasef Kamal, and Rasem Khalidi—turned out to be notorious German and Japanese agents. Khalidi's record was such that not even the usual diplomatic tolerance in cases involving official guests of the United Nations prevented the State Department from denying him a visa because of "his activities in Nazi Germany." No association with the Nazis, not even of a directly criminal nature, has been considered compromising in the Arab nationalist movement. To it, nothing had occurred that necessitated an intellectual and spiritual disassociation from Nazi ideas.

When one hears from incorrigible Nazi sympathizers promises of "exterminating" Israel and the Israelis, one had better take them literally rather than as mere figures of speech.

In such parts of the Arab world as the United Arab Republic, anti-Israeli campaigns bear a disquieting resemblance to the one-time products of Goebbels' Propaganda Ministry. This is not surprising, for many Nazi experts, not only on missiles but also on anti-Semitic propaganda, found haven and positions of importance in Nasser's UAR. Nasser's already mentioned friendly biographer, Robert St. John, confronts the issue:

> Naguib [the first titular President after Nasser's coup] had quietly appointed one of Adolf Hitler's economic experts, Dr. Wilhelm Voss, head of the Egyptian Central Planning Board and chief adviser to the War Ministry. Dr. Johann von Leers, who had been one of Goebbels' most trusted anti-Semitic rabble-rousers, was named political adviser to the Information Department. He had escaped from Germany to Argentina, where he had been publisher of a notorious German monthly, *Der Weg*, dedicated to perpetuating Hitler's ideas about Jews. The former Grand Mufti of Jerusalem had obtained the position in Cairo for him, and when he arrived, greeted him publicly, adding, "We thank you for venturing to take up the battle against the power of darkness that has become incarnate in world Jewry."
>
> Voss and Von Leers were only two. Every day additional names were whispered. Other foreigners might be trying to get out of Egypt, but the ex-Nazis were pouring in. There were hundreds of them, who saw in post-revolutionary Egypt a place they could fish in troubled waters. They changed their names so as not to embarrass their hosts. Von Leers became Sidi Mohamed Ali. Bernard Bender was known in the police circles in which he worked as Lieutenant Colonel Ben Salem. L. Moser, who helped organize an Egyptian youth movement, was called Colonel Hassan Suleiman. In the security force there was a Colonel al-Nahar, but his real name was Gleim. An adviser on publications was listed as Hassan al-Maan, although his passport said Buhle. Many of these men had been brought in by Farouk, but they were not unpopular with Free Officers like Anwar el Sadat, who had seen nothing wrong with Hitler except that he lost.[16]

---

16 St. John, *op. cit.*, pp. 152-153.

The above mentioned Gleim alias Ali al-Nahar is none other than SS-Standartenfuehrer (Colonel) Leopold Gleim, head of the Gestapo in war-occupied Poland, who is under the death sentence of a Polish court. In addition to his continued anti-Semitic literary preoccupations, Gleim now controls the Egyptian secret police as well as concentration camps for political prisoners. Under his police jurisdiction are also Egypt's Jews.

Lt. Colonel "Ben Salem" is none other than SS-Obersturmbannfuehrer Bernard Bender, who during World War II headed a special branch of the Gestapo which hunted Jewish resistance groups. He also served in occupied parts of the USSR. Bender, who now heads an organization of former Nazis living in the Arab countries, came to Egypt together with Dr. Hans Eisler, the notorious physician of the Buchenwald concentration camp, who also, as a judge in wartime Prague, sentenced 25 Czechs to death.

There is SS-General Oscar Dirlewanger, whose brigade ("Dirlewangerbrigade") specialized in wiping out partisans in Poland and the Ukraine, and who has the distinction of being responsible for Nasser's personal safety and presumably also for that of his guests, including Soviet President Nikolai Podgorny.

Among those who are training Egyptian "volunteers" for the Palestine Liberation Army are Erich Alten alias Ali Bella, former head of the Jewish Department of the Gestapo in Nazi-occupied Galicia; Willy Berner alias

Ben Kashir, an SS veteran from the Mathausen concentration camp; and Col. Baumann alias Ali ben Khader, one of the exterminators of the Warsaw Ghetto.

Among those who now supervise or help in Egypt's anti-Israeli and anti-Jewish propaganda are Franz Buensche, one-time official of Goebbel's Propaganda Ministry, and author of such books as *Sexual Crimes of the Jews;* and Louis Heiden, also a veteran of Goebbel's ministry and now the translator and distributor of Hitler's *Mein Kampf* in Arabic. How well he acquits himself of his new assignment is attested to by the fact that during Israel's 1956 Sinai campaign it emerged that Egyptian officers had been receiving an Arabic translation of *Mein Kampf* as part of their standard army issue.[17]

There are scores of others we know by name, position in the Nazi apparatus and position in the Nasser apparatus. There are scores of war criminals wanted as such by the governments of formerly Nazi-occupied territories as well as by the others of the wartime allies. To list even those so known, who are but a minority of that type of personnel that has been sought out by the Nasser regime, would require many additional pages of print.

These are the men helping to mold the new Egypt, the United Arab Republic.

Nazism was defeated militarily in Europe. The mili-

---

[17] *A Conspiracy of Complicity and Complacency* by David Porter, Vantage Press, New York, 1966, p. 122.

tary defeat was inescapably accompanied by an ideological defeat. Even the most unrepenting of its adherents had to make theoretical adjustments—enough to be referred to as *neo*-Nazi. But this was not necessarily the case in the Nazi ideological periphery, where old sentiments, not grossly undermined by a local drama of military capitulation, could survive without much change. This accounts for the continued strength of anti-Semitic and otherwise pro-Nazi movements in some Latin American countries. It also accounts for their strength in some Arab countries, particularly the United Arab Republic.

Expertise on Jews

The truth is that contrary to contradictory professions intended for export, it is not merely Zionism and Israel that are objects of popular and officially whipped-up hatred, but the Jews generally. Domestic propaganda in Arab countries, especially the UAR, reveals the presence of every anti-Semitic motif known in history. The argument of Arab spokesmen that as Semites themselves they cannot be anti-Semites is sheer demagoguery for at most it justifies no more than a terminological innovation that would more specifically identify hatred of Jews.

But more than any other influence, it was, and paradoxically continues to be, Nazism that has molded the Arab attitude toward the Jews in Israel and elsewhere. This influence is achieved through the close contacts between Arab leaders, groups and publications and their anti-Semitic counterparts in Germany and elsewhere. It is also achieved through the presence of the many Nazi experts in positions of influence in the UAR. And, last but not least, it is achieved through the undiminished momentum of deeply imbedded indigenous hatreds, prejudices and hysteria.

Anti-Semitic Arab propaganda uses the full arsenal of libel that has over the centuries accumulated against Jews anywhere. It ranges from the *Protocols of the Learned Elders of Zion* to the Arabic version of *Mein Kampf*, from Henry Ford's *The International Jew* to eulogies for Hitler as the avenger of Christ, from outworn misrepresentations of the Talmud to admiration for Adolf Eichmann as *shahid* or martyr.

The visit of Pope Paul VI to the Holy Land, occasioned a great deal of Arab preoccupation with Christian theology. In its coverage of the Pope's arrival in Jordan, Radio Amman included, on January 4, 1964, the following comment:

> Some two thousand years ago the Jews crucified Jesus, after beatings, humiliations and tortures that heap shame upon mankind everywhere. And fifteen years ago, in the most cruel manner, the Jews overran Palestine. They attacked its innocent, unarmed citizens and subjected many of them to the most villainous atrocities. . . .
>
> Thus the Jews prove their responsibility for the infamies of their forebears, and for the crucifixion and humiliation of Christ nineteen generations ago.

The Cairo press, too, had thoughts occasioned by the Pope's visit to the Holy Land. The prominent weekly

Akhbar el-Yom did not satisfy itself with solving a murder of two millenia ago; it also engaged in detective work on a more recent crime:

> Christianity holds fast to its belief that the Jews killed Christ—because they admitted their guilt and boasted of it, and because the way they treat Christians and everybody else is like that of bloodthirsty murderers. . . . And as for the claim these vagrants make—why do they trouble to clear themselves of something they admitted perpetrating two thousand years ago? Why are they so anxious to still their conscience over the blood of Christ, when so many fingers have pointed at them to claim the blood of Kennedy?[18]

The two-murder solution was not an *Akhbar el-Yom* exclusive; it was propagated from many forums and printed pages. Anis Mansur presented it with no less conviction in Cairo's *Al-Musawar*:

> . . . There is a definite trend among Catholics to exonerate the Jews completely from the blood of Jesus. . . . The Jews have already suffered dozens of times since those days. They pleaded innocence of this dastardly crime hundreds of times. What Hitler did to them was simply revenge for what they did to Christ. . . .
>
> Kennedy was a Catholic—and his assassin Jewish. The killer of Kennedy's assassin was Jewish, too, and so is the man in charge of the investigation.
>
> While the Catholics are busy making peace with the Jews—the Jews are assassinating the foremost Catholic lay personality in the world. . . .
>
> The capitalist regime in America tolerates the existence of Jewish gangs . . . and America pays the price . . . which this time was high. It is inevitable that anti-Jewish

---

18 *Akhbar al-Yom,* Cairo, Dec. 14, 1963.

> feeling—flickering at present—will turn into an open hatred as cruel as the bullet that struck Kennedy. . . .[19]

When it comes to the murder of U.S. Presidents (and Senators), it turns out that the Jews have a great deal of experience known to *The Scribe,* a monthly publication of the National Publication House in Cairo which appears in several language editions—English, French, German, Italian, and Spanish. Said that prominent UAR periodical in its April 1964 issue:

> At the risk of being accused of anti-semitism (sic), we want, in the single pursuit of truth, to prove that President Kennedy, just like the two American Presidents assassinated before him, was the victim of a Zionist-armed hand. It is no secret that John Wilkes Booth, murderer of President Abraham Lincoln, and Leon Czolgosz, who assassinated President McKinley, were both Jews in the service of the Zionist cause.

With all these Jewish killers of U.S. Presidents generously added to the Jewish fold, probably the most unwanted gift is one made by the Lebanese newspaper *Al-Nahar,* which in February 1964, identified President Johnson himself as a Jew. (Almost the first *good* reason for opposing Israel?)

Another Arab writer has figured out exactly why the Jews killed President Kennedy. Amin Sami al-Ghamrawi writes in a book that this was necessary for the Jews' "domination over the wealth of the American people," which we "learn," follows the Jewish pattern at least in three other nations. Writes the Arab scholar and historian:

---

[19] *Al Musawar,* Cairo, December 6, 1963.

> In Russia the Jews tried to steal the revolution when it was still in the cradle, and today they try to wreck the regime there. . . .
> In France the French people have no property whatsoever left; everything has gone to the Jews. The German people did not know that before Hitler tried to exterminate the Jews, he had been one of those who defended them.[20]

With so much "knowledge" accumulated about the Jews, elementary devotion to scholarship requires that adequate provisions be made for bestowing it to the younger generation. Soon it will be this younger generation that will man Sharm-el-Sheikh and other confrontation spots with Israel, and it is therefore of particular importance that it know the enemy. A British reporter's account proves that in fact much attention has been given to the educational needs of Arab children:

> . . . In the Gaza Strip . . . the Israel Army has collected a fearsome roomful of anti-Jewish paintings, which might have been produced by the SS and were in fact produced by 12-year-old Arab schoolgirls. . . . [21]

Another observer had opportunity to convince himself that Jordanian children receive an education, or what passes for such in some Arab lands, by no means inferior to that of the Gaza students. In Amman, he could "watch thirty or so children attending lessons at which they repeat after the teacher with rhythmic handclaps couplets vilifying the Jews."[22]

Formidable as Arab knowledge of the Jews, their

---

20 *Lihadha Ukirhu Israel* (This Is Why I Hate Israel) by Amin Sami al-Ghamrawi, Dar al-Nahda al-Arabiya, Cairo, 1964, p. 352.

21 David Marquand, *Manchester Guardian* (Weekly), July 13, 1967.

22 Harold Jackson, *Manchester Guardian* (Weekly), July 20, 1967.

history and character proves to be, it would not be in vain to expect equal expertise in the field of theoretical Judaism.

Expertise on Judaism

Not all Arab interest in theology is exhausted in preoccupation with Christianity; some is reserved for Judaism. In 1962, for example, Egypt's National Publishing House included in a series of "National Books" one on *Talmudic Human Sacrifices.* Even the introduction provides important "education":

> The Talmud believes that the Jews are made from different material from the rest of mankind, who are the servants and property of the Jews. . . . Their sages commanded them to ill-treat the rest of the nations, to kill their children, to suck their blood, and to take possession of their riches. (p. 7)

Another expert on the Jewish faith is Abdullah el-Tal, who had participated in the signing of the Armistice Agreement with Israel. In 1964, he published a book, in Cairo, *The Danger of World Judaism for Islam and Christianity.* On page 20, he "informs" the reader:

> The God of the Jews is not satisfied with the sacrifices of animals, but needs to be placated with human sacrifices. Hence the Jewish practice of slaughtering children and sucking their blood in order to mix it with unleavened bread for the Passover.

Al-Ahram, the semi-official Cairo newspaper that is edited by Nasser's close friend Mohamed Heikal, the ghost writer of his *The Philosophy of the Revolution,* and President of the Senate, had good news for the

Egyptian people on January 20, 1961:

> The Information Department of the United Arab Republic has been able to obtain copies of "The Protocols of the Elders of Zion," of the Talmud and other books. . . . The Department is now engaged in translating these books into Arabic, French and English in order to distribute them in African countries. . . . The Talmud says that whoever kills a non-Jew will be admitted to Paradise. The Talmud also permits the stealing of Gentile property and attacks upon the honor of non-Jewish women.

President Nasser himself was so impressed by the "education" he derived from the world's most compromised forgery that long before his Information Department prepared its translation and reprints of "The Protocols," he was personally distributing copies presumably obtained from other sources. The editor of the Indian magazine *Blitz*, R. K. Karanjia, published, on October 4, 1958, an interview with Nasser in which the Egyptian leader was quoted:

> I wonder if you have read a book called "Protocols of the Learned Elders of Zion." It is very important that you should read it. I will give you an English copy. It proves clearly, to quote from the Protocol, that "Three hundred Zionists, each of whom knows all the others, govern the fate of the European continent and they elect their successors from their entourage."

Indeed, so "important" did Nasser consider that "book" that on January 28, 1964, his representative at the Arab League session in Cairo proposed its renewed distribution in Asia and Africa.

But distribution confined to Asia and Africa is not quite sufficient when pearls of wisdom of theology-minded Arab politicians are involved. Moved by a spirit of magnanimity, and launching their own version of a foreign aid program, Arab representatives occasionally impart their knowledge of the Jews' divine cursedness even from the official forums of the United Nations. Jamil M. Baroody, the learned representative of Saudi Arabia, for example, lectured the U.N. General Assembly on July 17, 1967:

> It was in Jerusalem that Jesus labored and died. It was Saul of Tarsus, later known as the apostle Paul, who spread the new Christian faith which Mr. Ben Gurion still renounces. Jesus does not exist for Ben Gurion and therefore Jesus should have no place in Jerusalem. The Christians and Moslems, however, are to be tolerated in visiting their holy shrines for the revenue which will be gathered from them to fill Israel's coffers. But this time there will be no Jesus to drive money changers from the temple. What a shame, what a shame that Jerusalem should come to this.

Many Arab leaders, as one would expect, also have an attitude toward the extermination of six million Jews by the Nazis. They register no objection. Their reaction ranges from pretended disbelief to positive approval and regrets that the genocide was not total. President Nasser himself was quoted in an interview with the neo-Nazi *Deutsche National Zeitung und Soldatenzeitung* of Germany as having said:

> The lie of the six million murdered Jews is not taken seriously by anybody.[23]

On April 16, 1965, in an interview in that same neo-Nazi periodical, the UAR's Foreign Minister Mahmoud

---

[23] *Deutsche National Zeitung und Soldaten Zeitung,* May 1, 1964.

Riad was quoted:

> . . . most nations are not interested in these [Nazi crime] trials and [wish] that these nuisances be stopped. This self-flagellation does not bring honor to Germany. Often, it seems to me as though the Germans were begging to be slapped. What is referred to in Germany as pressure of world public opinion is in reality the pressure of a tiny minority . . .

Symptomatically, apologia-through-denial has been the favorite method of German neo-Nazis in confronting the genocide their nation has committed on the Jews. But, as among the German neo-Nazis so also among the Arabs, there are those who would not think of denying or decrying the macabre record. The Palestine Arab Delegation, for example, sent, in October 1961, a statement of the Grand Mufti in Jerusalem to all the U.N. delegations, which said in part:

> The enmity of Nazis to Jews . . . was based on well documented research and studies which showed that the Jews were a strong factor in bringing about the defeat of Germany in World War I and dominated the political, economic and professional life of Germany.

Still more ingenious was Hussein Dhu al-Figar, at the time Deputy Foreign Minister of the UAR, who on June 11, 1962, was quoted in Cairo's *Ruz al-Yusuf* as denying the murder of six million Jews by the Nazis and then adding:

> There are documents confirming the existence of Jewish gangs in Germany whose task it was to kill Jews in order to create sympathy for the Jews and Ben-Gurion himself was the leader of one of these gangs.

Perhaps most candid of the Arab voices on the Nazi extermination of Jews was Beirut's *Al Anwar*, which, on

June 9, 1960, published this caption with a cartoon:

> Ben Gurion: "You deserve the death penalty, because you killed six million Jews." Eichmann: "There are many who say I deserve the death penalty because I didn't manage to kill the rest."

Above is but a fraction of the available data. Even a fraction of that fraction coming from West Germany, would cause justified Soviet complaints of Nazi revival to be more urgent than they are already. But coming from the Middle East, they are not discerned for the dangers they pose.

There are, of course, in many countries political lunatics, paranoiacs whose "ideas" are quite similar to those quoted above. But the men quoted here are not ordinary lunatics nor even ordinary citizens in their countries. They are, in fact, leading and powerful personalities: the President of the largest Arab nation, Cabinet ministers, writers, prominent journalists. They not only speak for their countries, they also reflect their peoples' values.

But more than anything else, they betray their own peoples. For what the Arab nations need most are not anachronistic fanatics, social illiterates and political demagogues, but educators, genuine enlighteners who would not only replace the muscle of a camel with the motion of the engine, but also lift the minds, values and ethos of the people to more cultivated levels.

Every foreign effort to assist in such a process would be more than justified. But if instead I am called upon to accept the Arab people's present ideas, and if I am called upon to support *those* ideas in the name of anything that is progressive, socialist or revolutionary, then I opt out. Even if one should remain the only man on earth remembering what an aspiration to progress is, one would contribute more towards its realization than millions who, in the process of pursuing misguided theoretical consistency, wind up endorsing the spiritual inheritance of Nazism. If such be "progress," who would want to be "progressive?"

Arab Portraits and Self-portraits

No system whose theoretical premises include blind ethnic hatreds and religious prejudices, and which has an amazing rapport with Nazi criminals, can conceivably be progressive. And indeed one finds in the United Arab Republic a great many of the corollaries one would, as a matter of internal consistency, expect to find in a Nazi-inspired system.

Without purporting to analyze the nature of Nasser's revolution, we can nonetheless note a few significant characteristics, which bespeak its over-all internal trend. Symptomatic, for instance, is the fact that there are in the UAR thousands of political prisoners. (Radio Amman, on January 3, 1967, put their number at 50,000.)

No less symptomatic is the strict censorship of the press. Says Robert St. John in discussing Nasser's attitude and policy:

> He has no conception of what a free press means. For him

> the press is an instrument of government, to be used to advance a cause. Under his personal direction one of the most unpredictable censorship systems in the world has been set up in Cairo. Before a foreign radio reporter can make a broadcast he must submit seven copies of his script to a censor, who can delay approval until the foreigner has missed his air appointment or eliminate certain words and make the broadcaster say the opposite of what he intended, and it is forbidden to mention on the air that the script has been censored. Censorship of newspaper dispatches is blind: the correspondent does not know what has been excised . . .
>
> All newspaper and radio correspondents from abroad are closely watched, on his orders. Their telephones are tapped, their mail is opened, and they are often followed.
>
> Sometimes the entire Middle East section is ripped from incoming American news magazines before they are permitted on the stands. Every shop that makes microfilms is required to submit secretly to the censor anything a customer brings in, before photographing it.[24]

An international incident, which toward the end of 1964 attracted world-wide attention, epitomizes the quality of the prevailing government in Cairo, precisely because it synthesizes indigenous efforts and Nazi talents. We are recalling the notorious Louk Affair, the case in which Egyptian diplomats tried to abduct from Italy an Israeli citizen, Mordekai Louk, in a weirdly equipped trunk. It later emerged (from the testimony of Shariff Shaker, a former Egyptian information officer residing in Paris, as well as from other sources) that the trunk had been built by former SS-Colonel Helmut Harbinger; that it had been used on numerous occa-

[24] St. John, *op. cit.,* p. 239.

sions; and that at least in one case Nasser was personally present to receive the human cargo as the trunk was being unloaded in Cairo. Well, one must admit to having semantic difficulty in accepting progressive characterizations of the UAR despite such events.

Certainly, the repeatedly reported use of poison gases by the Egyptian forces against Yemeni villages is a measure of the political morality that prevails in Cairo.

Actually, considering the philosophy and personnel of government, the use of poison gas is less surprising than the fact that few people seem to remember that Egypt is, for all practical purposes, a dictatorship of a military junta, with all the characteristics of such government. Even fewer seem to be aware that the "progressive" United Arab Republic is also a theocracy with a constitutionally established religion, namely that of Islam.

The status of Islam as a state religion is directly in keeping with Nasser's personal vision of the Arab future—indeed it is a mere beginning in a much more ambitious theocratic dream:

> When I went with the Egyptian delegation to the Kingdom of Sa'udi Arabia to offer condolences on the death of its great sovereign, my belief in the possibility of extending the effectiveness of the Pilgrimage, building upon the strength of the Islamic tie that binds all Muslims, grew very strong. I stood before the Ka'ba, and in my mind's eye I saw all the regions of the world which Islam has reached. Then I found myself saying that our view of the Pilgrimage must change. . . . It should become an

> institution of great political power and significance. . . . When I consider the 80 million Muslims in Indonesia, and the 50 million in China, and the millions in Malaya, Siam and Burma, and the nearly 100 million in the Middle East, and the 40 million in the Soviet Union, together with other millions in far-flung parts of the world—when I consider these hundreds of millions united by a single creed, I emerge with a sense of the tremendous possibilities which we might realize . . . enabling them and their brothers in faith to wield power wisely and without limit.[25]

This is hardly a revolutionary, socialist or progressive mind talking. This is a dark theocratic brain dreaming of a world-wide caliphate. Nor is there in that vision of grandeur room for any meaningful social content, but only for grandeur for its own and religion's sake. This is a crusader of the Middle Ages sounding off anachronistically in the twentieth century.

As for Syria's claim to socialism, its genuineness is alternately confirmed or rejected by the UAR itself, depending on the passing political season. For one period the voice of a Cairo newspaper was typical:

> Today we know that the Ba'ath party wants a Nazi, fascist regime that will give its members freedom to impose their will on the masses who are of no significance to the Ba'ath leaders.[26]

There is reason for communists and everybody else who is not a Ba'ath party member to share this evaluation, for Ba'ath is Syria's only legal party.

One cannot conclude this quick glance at the political map of the Middle East without a capsule impression

---

25 Nasser, *op. cit.*, pp. 111-114.

26 *Akhbar el-Yom,* Cairo, June 2, 1963.

of the Jordanian kingdom, the state which is probably the most artificial imperialist state creation in history. There neither is nor ever was a Jordanian ethnic group, culture or history. Nor has there ever existed a national Transjordanian movement among the occupants of the real estate that was to become Transjordan (later Jordan). The whole of it is a British invention even more than the Saigon regime is an American invention. Its regal dynasty is a British import; its armed forces have been created as a British military appendage; its very nationhood was nothing but a British colonial convenience. Yet somehow, when viewed in its confrontation with Israel, all that is true about Jordan is miraculously transferred to Israel, while the Jordanian origin is no obstacle to acceptance as an authentic force of national liberation.

The longer one observes Arab countries the more one discovers symptoms of political backwardness, religious intolerance and ideas rooted in dated traditions, which are incompatible with any modern society, least of all with one aspiring to social justice. This generalization holds true despite the truly significant differences between one Arab country and another.

But this sobering realization gives no grounds for a negative attitude toward the Arab peoples; it is a challenge. It tells us how desperately these nations need progress and political rejuvenation. To hide this from them and instead to flatter their present political life as progressive, socialist and/or revolutionary is the worst disservice to them. In effect, it contributes to the prevention of their progress.

Much as we have concentrated on exposing the non-progressive character of predominant components of the Arab nationalist movement, the compromised picture that emerges does not diminish even one iota the Arabs' right to be free and to act for their self-advancement. Such basic rights hardly depend on the acceptability of their philosophical values and political ideas to anyone. As nothing the Arabs invoke entitles them to deny life and prosperity to Israelis, ugly Arab politics entitles no one to deny life and prosperity to Arabs. Human life is justified by virtue of existence and needs no additional justification. Any just solution of the Arab-Israeli conflict must proceed from this assumption.

Jewish Nationalism

M. S. Arnoni

Between Moses and Marx

That Jewish nationalism, commonly known as Zionism,[27] should be considered a term of opprobrium in political quarters which otherwise support nationalist movements is no less strange than the progressive image bestowed today on the Middle Eastern inheritors of

[27] In East Europe, before the mass extermination of Jews in World War II, there were Jewish non-Zionist and anti-Zionist parties, which, too, in one measure or another, were nationalist. They ranged from autonomists (Folkists), who sought Jewish territorial autonomies in European countries, to Bundists, Marxist Socialists, who, having participated in the October Revolution, were eventually outlawed in the USSR, and who were firmly dedicated to the upholding of Yiddish, not Hebrew, culture. Their pre-eminent leaders in Poland, Dr. Henry Ehrlich and Victor Alter, were executed in 1941 after the Soviet Union had occupied parts of Poland in 1939.

Nazism. There are, of course, historic reasons for this paradox, but not everything that has a reason is justified. Yet, the sheer habit of attitudes is often so strong as to survive any challenge of rationality.

Those Marxists to whom Zionism is anathema would have difficulty imagining any Zionists as participating in the October Revolution. Yet, it does not take imagination but mere information to know that such was the case and that some Zionists (Poale Zion–Left) remained for years legally organized in the Soviet Union. In fact, theirs was one of the last, if not the last, non-Bolshevik party to be dissolved, having outlived both the Mensheviks and the Social Revolutionaries. Yes, there have always been Zionists who also considered themselves Marxists, and their position in the Zionist movement as well as in Israel's political and social life is prominent indeed.

Some people fail to appreciate that the Zionist camp stretches over a political spectrum ranging from the extreme right to the extreme left. Included are many who differ from other communists only by ties to Palestine and the Jewish national home. The Zionist communal and cooperative movements in Israel have such strength that they are a source of inspiration to various socialist and other movements, especially in Asia and Africa. Nor is it an accident that among the Israeli leaders in virtually every field of public life preeminence goes to members of as purely communistic settlements as are in existence anywhere.

There is nothing surprising about this, for from its very beginning the Jewish resettlement experiment has been conducted by socialists of all creeds, including avowed Marxists. One of Marx's contemporaries and associates, Moses Hess, was a theoretician of both socialism and Zionism. There were many others, including such disciplined Marxist thinkers as Ber Borochov and such apostles of collectivist life and a "Religion of Labor" as A. D. Gordon.

The incompatibility between Zionism and communism emerges upon closer examination as nothing truly basic. It is tactical rather than one of principles. But even tactically derived attitudes can with passage of time become frozen.

Zionism's principal postulate is to solve the Jewish problem through the territorial concentration of the Jews. The choice of country in which this concentration was to take place was secondary and for many years led to controversies within the Zionist camp. With the Soviet Union itself having at various phases favored Jewish colonization in the Ukraine, Crimea and at last Biro-Bidjan, the principle of territorial concentration of Jews did not, in itself, divide the Zionists and communists. It was rather the particular territory chosen for Jewish settlement that has caused a fatal rift. But the communist argument against Jewish settlement in Palestine had nothing to do with "artificiality"; obviously, the Jews were indigenous to Biro-Bidjan no more than they were to Palestine.

The irreconcilability had rather to do with the naive, romantic and illusionary stage through which communists had to pass before holding power anywhere and in the years following their first successful revolution. The thought that any unresolved problem would survive the communist solutions was an intolerable heresy. Communism was a panacea. It was going to solve everything and anything that needed solution. Jails, for example, would disappear from the communist society, for the causes of crime would be removed. Hatred, envy and strife would have no room in the classless society. Racial discrimination was absolutely unimaginable. As for the Jews, all their problems, suffering, persecution, second-class citizenship would, without a shadow of a doubt, be gone together with the system that profited from them. The Jewish question would no longer exist. Of course, if the Jews should want to preserve their historic cultural-ethnic uniqueness, they would be welcome to do so, for communism grants complete equality to all nationalities. An autonomous Jewish region will be provided.

To suggest that any problem needed a solution outside the communist framework or beyond the territorial boundaries of its reign was tantamount to non-confidence in communism itself. Why would anyone look outside the country preparing itself for socialism and communism as if they did not suffice for curing all the social ills? As only counter-revolutionaries would imagine crime surviving the capitalist system, so would

The two greatest Arab heroes: the ***Fuehrer and the ex-Mufti.***

"To His Eminence the Grand Mufti in remembrance, July 4, 1943, H. Himmler."

Mufti is welcomed to Croatia by Cabinet members of the Ustashi regime.

Inseparable friends: Presidents Tito and Nasser.

Other friends: Nasser, Naguib and the Mufti in joint prayer.

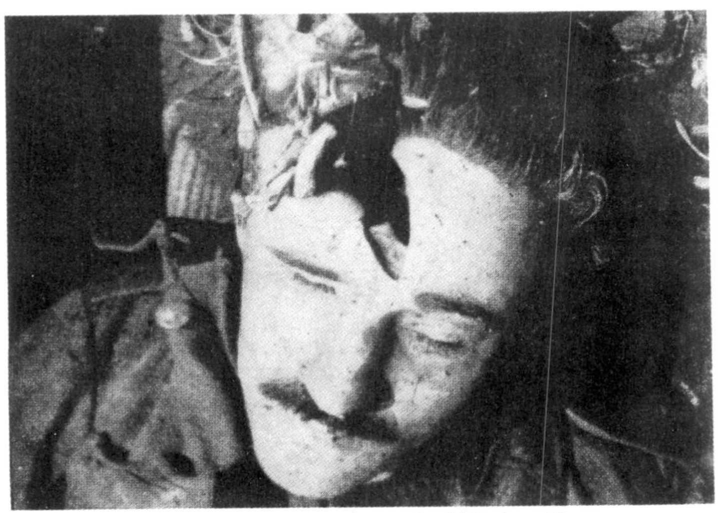

A Tito partisan executed by Mufti-recruited Moslem SS-men.

Warsaw Ghetto, 1943.

Hitler's Mein Kampf *in Arabic.*

Arab refugee camp in the Gaza Strip.

...يث عن الحاج أمين الحسيني مفتي فلسطين

...لحة التي لم يرسلها سماحته إلى المجاهدين وابقاها في الزيتون .. وقصص اخرى

من السبت الى السبت

بقلم محمد التابعي

نوى ان اخصص مقال اليوم للحديث عن اليمن وعن الجسر البحرى الذى اقمناه منذ عام ـ اى فى اوائل اكتوبر عام ١٩٦٢ اه بيننا وبين اليمن ونقلنا عليه او به آلافا من الجنود ومئات الأطنان من السلاح والذخيرة والعتاد . . وهذا كله فى ايام معدودات . .

وكانت معجزة . . . والحديث فيها طويل . . فى هذا كنت اريد ان اكتب هذا الاسبوع . .

ولكن مقالا بقلم الزميل الصديق ناصر النشاشيبى اغرانى بالعودة الى الحديث عن فلسطين . .

ولقد كنت كففت عن الكتابة فى قضية او ماساة فلسطين .. لان الماساة شبعت حتى طفحت من كثرة ما كتب ونشر وما قيل فيها نثرا ونظما ... ولو كان النثر والنظم يستطيعان ان يردا الحقوق الى اصحابها لكان عرب فلسطين قد استعادوا اوطانهم ودورهم وممتلكاتهم منذ سنوات ... وكانوا قد طهروا الارض المقدسة والقوا بعصابات اليهود فى البحر .

لا اكتب عن هؤلاء

الحاج امين الحسيني

عبد الرحمن عزام

Cairo's Akhbar el-Yom, *October 12, 1963, accusing the Mufti of inciting Arabs to flee Palestine in 1948.*

نداء من مجلس عمال حيفا

الى سكان حيفا العرب .

الى العمال والموظفين .

لقد مرت على حيفا فترة طويلة من الزمن ، عشنا وعشتم فيها تحت ظلال الطمأنينة والاخوه والتفاهم والتعاون . فازدهر هذا البلد المشترك وازدهرت حالة سكانه يهوداً وعرباً . حتى اصبح نموذجاً لباقي البلدان .

وعلى حين غرة انقلبت الحال واثيرت بيننا وبينكم فتناً دموية طالما حذرناكم من مثيريها وانذرناكم من عواقبها الوخيمه .

اما اليوم والحمد لله فقد طهرت المدينة من عوامل السوء وفر المشاغبون خوف من ان تنالهم يد العدالة . وارتفع عنا نير الاستعمار .

فبات هذا البلد يسوده الامن وتعمه الطمأنينة . وانفتح فيه المجال ثانية لتقارب بين السكان والتعاون بين العمال والحصول على الرزق الحلال

ان المخاوف التي غرسها المشاغبون في صدوركم لا اساس لها من الصحه اننا قوم نحب السلم ولا نضمر الشر للاهلين المسالمين الذين يدأبون مثلنا على العمل الشريف والسعي المثمر فلا تخافوا . لا تخربوا بيوتكم بايديكم . لا تقطعوا ارزاقكم بانفسكم ، ولا تجلبوا على انفسكم مشقات الرحيل وعذاب الجلاء .

اعلموا انكم اذا رحلتم فلا ينتظركم سوى الفقر والمذله والاحتقار . اما هنا في حيفا فالباب امامكم مفتوح للعودة الى اعمالكم والمحافظه على بيوتكم واموالكم وراحة عيالكم واطفالكم .

فيا ايها السكان المسالمين

ان مجلس عمال حيفا اي فرع الهستدروت في هذا البلد ينصحكم بالبقاء . ويدعوكم للرجوع الى اعمالكم الاعتياديه . اننا مستعدون لمساعدتكم على اعادة الامور الى مجاريها الحسنه . وتسهيل الحصول على حاجيات المعيشه . وفتح ابواب العمل بوجوهكم . وادخال الطمأنينة في قلوبكم

فيا ايها العمال ان بلدنا المشترك حيفا يدعوكم الى التعاون معنا على تعميره وترقيته ، وازدهاره وتقدمه . فلا تخونوه ولا تخونوا انفسكم ، كونوا على بصيرة من امركم وسيروا الى سبيل الخير والسعادة فذلك خير لكم .

النقابة العامة للعمال اليهود (الهستدروت)
مجلس عمال حيفا

حيفا ٢٨-٤-٤٨

קול קורא מאת מועצת פועלי חיפה

אל תושבי חיפה הערבים
אל הפועלים והפקידים

שנים על שנים חיינו יחד בעירנו חיפה בבטחון ובתוך יחסי הבנה ואחוה, הודות לכך פרחה והתפתחה עירנו לטובת התושבים היהודים והערבים ושימשה מופת ליתר ערי הארץ.

גורמים עויינים לא יכלו שאת את המצב הזה, והם אשר סכסכו וקלקלו את היחסים בינינו וביניכם, אך יד הצדק השיגה אותם. עירנו טוהרה מגורמים אלה, אשר ברחו על נפשם ועתה שוב הושלטו סדר ובטחון בעיר ונפתחה דרך לחדוש יחסי שתוף והתקרבות בין התושבים והפועלים היהודים והערבים לחיים תקינים.

עתה הננו רואים צורך לאמר לכם גלויות: עם אוהב שלום אנחנו! אין כל יסוד לפחד אשר מטילים עליכם. אין בלבנו שינאה וכוונות רעות כלפי התושבים שוחרי השלום האמונים כמונו על עבודה ויצירה. אל פחדו! אל תחריבו את בתיכם במו ידיכם אל תסתמו את מקורות פרנסתכם ואל תמיטו על עצמכם אסונות בעקב פנוי וטלטולים שלא לצורך. בעקבות הטלטולים ישיגוכם עוני והשפלה, אך בעירנו-עירכם חיפה פתוחים לפניכם השערים לעבודה, לחיים ושלום לכם ולמשפחותיכם.

תושבים ישרים ושוחרי שלום!

מועצת פועלי חיפה וההסתדרות מיעצים לכם ולטובתכם להשאר בעיר ולחזור לעבודתכם הרגילה אנו מוכנים לבוא לעזרתכם בהחזרת החיים למסלולם הטוב, להקל עליכם בהשגת מצרכי אכל, לפתוח בפניכם מקומות עבודה.

פועלים!

עירנו המשותפת חיפה קוראת אתכם להשתתף בבנינה, קידומה ופיתוחה. אל תבגדו בה ואל תבגדו בעצמכם. ראו את עיניכם נכוחה ולכו בדרך הטוב והישר

ההסתדרות הכללית של העובדים העברים בא"י
מועצת פועלי חיפה

חיפה 28.4.48

Arabic-Hebrew poster of the Haifa (Jewish) Workers' Council, April 28, 1948, appealing to Arabs to remain in their homes and jobs.

APPEAL BY THE HAIFA WORKERS' COUNCIL

TO THE ARAB RESIDENTS OF HAIFA
TO THE WORKERS AND OFFICIALS

For years we lived together in our city, Haifa, in security and in mutual understanding and brotherhood. Thanks to this, our city flourished and developed for the good of both Jewish and Arab residents, and thus did Haifa serve as an example to the other cities in Palestine. Hostile elements have been unable to reconcile themselves to this situation and it has been these elements which have induced conflicts and undermined the relations between you and us. But the hand of justice has overcome them. Our city has been cleared of these elements who fled for their lives. Thus, once again, does order and security prevail in the city and the way has been opened for the restoration of cooperation and fraternity between the Jewish and Arab workers.

At this juncture we believe it necessary to state in the frankest terms: We are peace-loving people! There is no cause for the fear which others try to instill in you. There is no hatred in our hearts nor evil in our intentions towards peace-loving residents who, like us, are bent upon work and creative effort.

Do not fear! Do not destroy your homes with your own hands; do not block off your sources of livelihood; and do not bring upon yourself tragedy by unnecessary evacuation and self-imposed burdens. By moving out you will be overtaken by poverty and humiliation. But in this city, yours and ours, Haifa, the gates are open for work, for life, and for peace, for you and your families.

UPRIGHT AND PEACE-LOVING WORKERS:

The Haifa Workers' Council and the Histadrut advise you for your own good to remain in the city and to return to your normal work. We are ready to come to your help, in restoring normal conditions, to assist you in obtaining food supplies, and to open up job opportunities.

WORKERS: OUR JOINT CITY, HAIFA, CALLS UPON YOU TO JOIN IN ITS UPBUILDING, ITS ADVANCEMENT, ITS DEVELOPMENT. DO NOT BETRAY YOUR CITY AND DO NOT BETRAY YOURSELVES. FOLLOW YOUR TRUE INTERESTS AND FOLLOW THE GOOD AND UPRIGHT PATH.

Federation of Jewish Labor in Palestine

THE HAIFA WORKERS' COUNCIL

Translation of the poster on the facing page.

"Socialist" education in Syria: a textbook cover.

The work of Arab infiltrators in Israel.

The work of Arab infiltrators in Israel.

Rome, Nov. 17, 1964: A policeman looks at the trunk, in which Egyptian diplomats tried to air-freight Mordekai Louk to Cairo.

Cairo, May 29, 1967: "We want war!"

مكتوم جـدا

رقم النسخه (٤)

قيادة لواء الامام علي بن ابي طالب
(المنيساه)

الرقم – م/١/١/١
التاريخ – ٧ حزيران ١٦٦

امر عمليات خاص لعملية (رعد)

خرائط المراجعه

القدس ٥ رام الله ٥ سلفيت ٥ صور
اللـد ٥ بالقياس ١/ ٠٠٠ر٥٠

الى – قائد كتيبة احتياط اللواء/ ٢٢

١. الموقف

أ. العدو

(١) لواء العدو في مستعمرة موتسا (١٦٤٧١٣٤٢) يسكن هذه المستعمرة حوالي ٨٠٠ شخصا يعملون بالزراعة ويقوم قسم منهم بحراسة المستعمرة.

(٢) تحرس المستعمرة خمسة والاف ليليه حولها.

(٣) يوجد خنادق محفوره حول المستعمرة وتحتل عند الحاجه.

(٤) المستعمرة محاطة بالاسلاك الشائكه.

(٥) مبانيه من الاسمنت وسقوف بعض بيوتها بالقرميد الاحمر.

(٦) تحتاج قوة المستعمرة من ٥–٧ دقائق للمقاتله واحتلال المراكز عند المفاجاة.

(٧) مراكز العدو القريبه من المستعمرة والتي يمكن ان تتدخل في المعركه للنجده.

(أ) معسكر القسطل (١٦٣١٣٢) قوة سرية مشاة مع السلاح مساندة وموقعها الدفاعي في المربع (١٦٣٧١٣٣٢).

(ب) معسكر شنيللر (١٢٠١٣٢) به سرية كتف اللواء السادس.

(ج) معسكر ابو غوش (١٦٠٠١٣٤١) قوة سرية حدود.

(٨) السيطرة الجويه لصالح العدو.

ب. قواتنا

(١) قصد قيادة الجبهه الغربيه القيام بعملية اغارة على مستعمرة (موتسا) وتدميرها وقتل من فيها.

(٢) اسند هذا الواجب الى قائد لواء الامام علي بن ابي طالب والذي بدوره اعطى هذه المهمة الى قائد كتيبة احتياط اللواء.

مكتوم جدا

Order for the destruction of Motza and the killing of all its inhabitants.

TOP SECRET

Copy No. 4

H.Q. IMAM ALY BEN ABI TALEB Brigade
(Operations)

Registration No.: A'1/1/1
Date : 7th June 1966

Special Operational Order "Operation (RA'AD)"
Ref. Maps:
Jerusalem, Ramallah, Salfit
Ag'ur, Lud, Yafo--Tel-Aviv
1:50000

To: Commander Reserve Battalion 27th Brigade.

1. Situation.

A. Enemy.

1) The enemy forces in MOTZA Colony (16471342). The inhabitants number about 800 persons, engage in agriculture and have guard details in the colony.

2) The colony mans five night guard-positions around it.

3) The colony is surrounded by slit-trenches which are manned when necessary.

4) The colony has barbed-wire fences.

5) The houses of the colony are built of concrete, and some have red-tile roofs.

6) The forces of the colony need 5-7 minutes to man their positions from the moment of surprise.

7) Enemy camps close to the colony which can take part in the campaign and advance reinforcements:--

a) CASTEL Camp (163133) one Infantry Co. with support detachments The defence position of this unit is on the hill (16371337).

b) SHNELLER Camp (170132) 6th Brigade Reconaissance Co.

c) ABU GOSH Camp (16301349) Border Police Co.

8) Air superiority to enemy.

B. Own Forces:

1) The intention of H.Q. Western Front is to carry out a raid on MOTZA Colony, to destroy it and to kill all its inhabitants.

2) This task was allocated to the Brigadier of the IMAM ALY BEN ABI TALEB Brigade who will further it to the Brigade Reserve Battalion.

../2

Translation of the order on the facing page.

الجمهورية العربية المتحدة
قيادة المنطقة الشرقية الجويـة
مكتب رئيس الاركان

" سـري للغايـة "

التيـد : ١٩٦٧/٣/٣٥/
التاريخ : ١٩٦٧/٥/١٦

أمر قتـال رقم ٦٧/٣

١ـ من المنتظر القيام بعمليات تعرضية لعزل منطقة النقب الجنوبي واحتلال ايـــــلات .

٢ـ تخصص المجهود الجوى التالى لاستخدامه بواسطة قائد القوات البرية لصالح العمليـة .

أـ ٢٧ طلعة سرب قاذف مقاتل من الالوية الجوية ٢ ، ١٢ المتمركزان حاليا فـــى القاعدتان ٢٥٦ ، ٢٤٨ .

بـ ٣ طلعة سرب قاذف خفيف من اللواء الجوى ٦١ المتمركز بالقاعدة ٢٢٩ .

ـ كما تخصص طلعة سرب قاذف ثقيل من احتياطى قائد القوات الجوية والدفـاع الجوى لصالح العملية . تطلب بمعرفة قائد القوات الجوية والدفاع الجوى .

٣ـ الحد الأقصى للمجهود اليومى :

ـ ٦ طلعة سرب قاذف مقاتل ، طلعة سرب قاذف خفيف .

٤ـ سوف تطلب الطلعات مباشرة بواسطة جماعة المعاونة الجوية من المطارات وستكـــون الخرقة .. مستمعة على نفس التردد .

٥ـ سيقوم بالتوجيه/على الاهداف ضباط توجيه من نقط توجيه متقدمة . ستخطر التشكيـلات الجوية بأسمائها الكودية والترددات اللاسلكية التى تعمل عليها فى حينـه .

٦ـ الالوان الكودية للتشكيلات الجوية أثناء توجيه الطائرات على الاهداف :

أـ الطائرات التى ستقوم بالعمل فى معاونة الاتجاه الرئيسى ورمزهـا الكودى (احمر)
بـ " " " " " " " الثانوى (ايلات) رمزها الكودى (أصفر)
جـ " " " " " فى عزل ميدان المعركة ورمزهـا الكـــودى (أخضر)

٧ـ ستقوم القوات الجوية بضرب مطار ايلات وضرب محطة الارسال ومستودعات البترول بهـا بمجهود مخصص لذلك من قيادة القوات الجويـة .

لواء طيار/ عبد الحميد عبد السلام دغيدى
قائد المنطقة الشرقيـة الجويـة
( )

Photostat of Battle Order No. 3 of the Egyptian Air Force dated 18 May 1967, relating to the air operations for the conquest of the southern Negev and cutting off Elat.

Egyptian battle order, dated May 18, 1967.

TOP-SECRET

U.A.R.
Eastern Area Command H.Q.
Chief of Staff's Bureau
No. td/3/1967/124
Date: 18 May 1967

BATTLE ORDER NO. 3/67

1. An offensive operation is planned for the cutting off of the southern Negev area and to conquer Eilat.

2. The following air power will be allocated for exploitation by the Ground Forces O.C. for the benefit of the operation.
   a. 27 fighter-bombardment squadron sorties from 2 and 12 Air Brigades stationed at 2 bases, Nos. 248 and 249.
   b. 3 light bomber squadron sorties by Air Brigade 61 from Base No. 229.
   --and a sortie of heavy bombing squadron from the reserves of the Air Force O.C. and Air Defence, for the benefit of the operation. Decided upon at the Conference of the Air Force O.C. and Air Defence.

3. MAXIMUM DAILY EFFORT
   --9 fighter-bombardment squadron sorties and a light bomber squadron sortie.

4. The sorties will be ordered directly through the Air Support Units at the air bases. Ops Room No. 50 will monitor the same frequency.

Bombing directions will be effected by the Air Support Liaison officers from forward control points.
   --Code names and radio frequencies will be given to the air formations at the time.

6. Color code formation designations to be used for directing planes to targets--
   a. Primary target support planes -- Red
   b. Secondary target support planes -- Yellow
   c. Planes acting to seal off the battle area -- Green

7. Air forces will bomb Eilat air field, the radio station, and the oil storage areas in an effort designated for that purpose by the Air Forces O.C.

(signed) LIWA (General) PILOT
Abd El Hamid Abd Al Salaam Daghidi
O.C. Eastern Air Command

Translation of the order on the facing page.

A toilet built of tombstones from a Jewish cemetery in Israel-occupied Jordan territory.

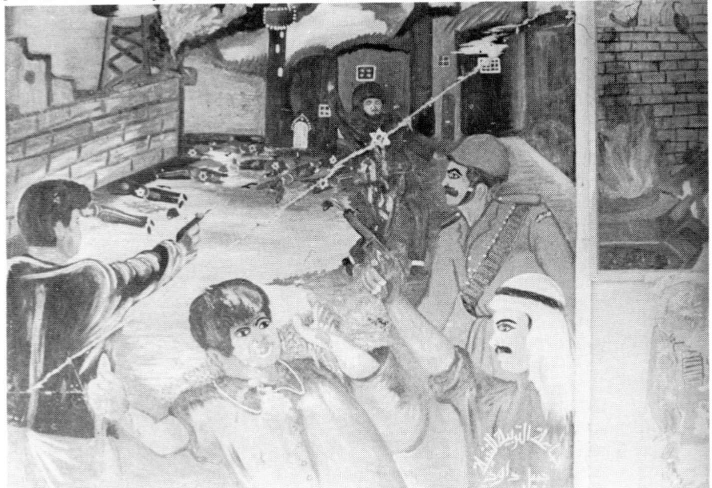

Paintings by children in the Gaza Strip depicting anti-Israeli revenge.

only counter-revolutionaries nostalgically look toward Palestine.

While this attitude provided the perennial negative emotions of much of the communist movement towards Israel, there were also more concrete reasons behind the hostility which was articulating itself. A Soviet Union bearing so recent memories of over a million interventionist foreign troops on her soil, surrounded by mortal enemies who would spare no effort to effect a downfall of the communist regime, harassed, ostracized, boycotted—to such a Soviet Union the idea of letting a large part of its citizenry maintain continual political contacts with political parties abroad was inconceivable, if for no other reason than state security. Yet, Zionist activities would necessarily involve close and massive liaison between the Jewish communities in the Soviet Union and those elsewhere.

Thus there was nothing ideologically incompatible between communism and Zionism, and the reason for the former's non-acceptance of the latter was one of political geography rather than theoretical contradiction. The Soviet Union was not hostile toward the idea of Jewish territorial concentration, and she had nothing against Palestine serving that purpose other than it being outside the Soviet orbit. Had Moses led the Jews to the Crimea or Biro-Bidjan, thus establishing a geographic attachment that would last for millenia, the Soviets' own Jewish policy would have been called "Zionism," and rather than being presented as reactionary it would now be cited as proof of complete communist equality of rights for national entities. But Moses seems to have lacked the stamina for a longer journey.

To some people the very idea of a Jewish state connotes a theocracy. Why should a religious group seek to have its own political entity? Such people seem to know little about the Jews, their history and culture. The overwhelming majority of the Jews consider themselves tied to each other not only by religion. With a sense of a common past, enduring loyalty and a destiny in which one Jewish community affects other Jewish communities, they consider themselves to be a peoplehood. In East Europe, few have ever questioned this, and the Soviet Union officially recognizes the Jews as a "nationality." Israel's being a Jewish state is no different from France's being a French state and China's being a Chinese state.

That certain Israeli laws, such as that bestowing immediate citizenship on Jews arriving in the country, are ethnically exclusive may be wise or not. But to construe this as a sign of racism is to be oblivious to the deliberate process of ingathering. What kind of a discovery is it that Zionism has never been a Greek, Indian or Peruvian movement but one of the Jews—intended as an answer to *their* problems? If that be racism, then every national budget, language and law constitutes racism, for each of them is intended to meet the needs of a *specific*, yes, exclusive, group of people.

There is, however, a difference between Israel's being a Jewish state—a phenomenon no less and no more legitimate than that of all ethnic states—and its theocratic encroachments. True, the religious jurisprudence in personal civil matters applies to each denomination autonomously and therefore does not constitute religious discrimination *per se*, but it nonetheless constitutes a very dark blemish on Israel's progressive image. It is a phenomenon for which one must have no more understanding, or tolerance, than when it occurs in any other country. Certainly, Israel should not compete with Franco's Spain in refusing to separate church and state. It is the less forgivable, because the vast majority of the Israelis are secular in orientation and the theocratic practices are imposed by a minority expediently courted for reasons of governmental coalition politics. However, the theocratic minority is not the only political force available for securing a parliamentary majority in Israel, where no party has an absolute majority and where, incidentally, political fragmentation serves as a little appreciated but highly refreshing dike against the conformity of one and two-party systems.

To be sure, theocratic encroachments are by no means the only bad side of Israeli life. But least of all are we here called upon to engage in a discussion of whatever we find objectionable in that country, just so as to prove our "objectivity." The pluses and minuses of the Israeli society are not germane to a discussion of its right of existence. We touched on the theocratic influences only because they do relate to the at times questioned normalcy of Israel's being a *Jewish* state.

But no matter what the degree of justification in any criticism of Israeli life, the most that can come of it are recommendations of correction and improvement, not an argument for dissolution. The premise that a society's shortcomings can justify its annihilation would be an advocacy of genocide. Significantly, those who criticize one aspect or another of Israeli society, presenting this as an argument for its dissolution, are not likely to display a similar disproportion between "crime and punishment" when other nations are involved. Least of all are they likely to favor the liquidation of the United Arab Republic, for instance, because the theocratic encroachments in it are incomparably greater than in Israel.

Legitimized Anti-Semitism

Whatever the origins of communists' hostility toward Jewish nationalism, the very existence of that hostility put into motion self-perpetuating psychological factors. Many a Jewish communist felt, for example, that he had to lean over backward to demonstrate his revolutionary loyalty by subordinating to it any ethnic sentiment. In this there has been quite an admixture of that self-hatred which is bound to afflict some members of any group suffering from discrimination.

To some degree communists' attack on Zionism provided vicarious fulfilment to people whose ideological consistency was not so complete as to cure them of the last vestiges of unadmitted anti-Semitism. The designation of "Zionism" provided a pretext for pouring out invective actually intended for the Jews.

While this has been true for decades, it seems to have gained special force in the present attitude of some communists toward Israel. Soviet zeal in opposing Israel provided the opportunity for many an unadmitted East European anti-Semite at last to find a respectable outlet for long frustrated emotions. Centuries-old East-European anti-Semitism could not possibly disappear overnight with the magic touch of a newly embraced communist ideology. To be sure, the Pole, Hungarian or Slovak, who since the end of World War II considers himself to be a communist, is aware of the incompatibility between anti-Semitism and communism. That is why he has not thought himself to be an anti-Semite and perhaps sincerely tried to overcome any contradictory bias. But this necessarily led to frustration, to a discrepancy between theoretical conviction and environmentally acquired impulses. Vehement Soviet support of Arab leaders who speak of "exterminating" Israel provided an excellent opportunity for releasing frustrated emotions.

One wonders how much popular acumen in international politics and how much of spontaneous, if secret, anti-Semitic emotions were reflected in the enthusiasm with which a Polish audience responded to communist leader Wladyslaw Gomulka's warning that his Jewish compatriots not form a "fifth column" by sympathizing with Israel. These emotions are nonetheless the leftovers of what in the Nazi-occupied land had animated an amazing degree of local collaboration in the extermination of Jews. How convenient and reassuring must it be for many at long last to be able to let their anti-Jewish feelings swing freely again without the embarrassment of thinking themselves or of being thought by others as reactionaries.

Even if anti-Semitic stereotypes were not discernible in much of what is presented as merely anti-Zionism, the demarcation line between hatred of Jews and hatred of Zionism may be much thinner than some people assume. True, not all the Jews are Zionists. Some Jews are as good, or better, at hating Zionism and Zionists as are some non-Jews. But this is no exceptional situation as nationalist movements go. No nationalist movement has ever spoken for all the members of its people. There were many Algerians, for instance, who collaborated with the French and opposed the independence struggle. French officials, could, and in fact did, point to such people as "proof" that they themselves were not against the Algerians and their aspirations, but merely against *some* Algerians and *some* of their aspirations. The same goes for Vietnam. By no means do all the Vietnamese identify with the National Liberation Front. There are some, like Marshal Ky, who welcome and encourage what the Americans are doing to their country and countrymen. The Americans point to these people to "prove" that they are not against the Vietnamese and their aspirations, but merely against some Vietnamese and some of their aspirations. Yet, unless one is either hopelessly gullible or intellectually corrupt, one must reject the U.S. definition of the Vietnamese national aspirations, some Vietnamese notwithstanding.

This is not merely a matter of statistics and majorities. A movement to be nationalist need not necessarily have popular majority support. Its political aspiration, not numerical support, determines whether it is nationalist. In fact, all nationalist movements start out as minority movements and history does not lack cases in which an independence movement has achieved popular majority support only *after* its ultimate victory. The United States of America is a case in point.

Least of all does this mean that such movements are not representative of their peoples. But acting as they do, not for one generation but for many, there is at no given time the opportunity available of polling all who are going to be affected by the struggle. In hindsight, when one adds up all the successive generations of their endorsers, it becomes clear that independence movements, even if acting for a particular generation's minority, do act for the *nation* and its generations-embracing majority. In the case of the Jews, however, not only is their nationalist movement representative even of the present generation, but a good case could be made for considering that movement supported morally, if tragically, also by the millions of recently exterminated Jews.

If we apply the truisms emerging from the general

experience of nationalist movements to the case of the Jews, then those who so vehemently protest that their anti-Zionism not be construed as anti-Jewishness would be more precise if they stated that, without opposing all the Jews and all their aspirations, they nonetheless oppose the Jewish national aspiration. They would then have to concede that in the case of the Jews they oppose precisely that which they believe to merit support in the case of all other peoples. They would then have to desist from claiming to favor all nationalist, independence and self-determination movements, and instead they would have to justify a double standard of judgment. In any case, they are now in the morally untenable position of denying to the Jews that which they would not think of denying to anyone else. The exception thus made is neither flattering nor beneficial to the individuals and peoplehood directly involved, and it is anti-Jewish in the very same sense in which the Black Feet movement was anti-Algerian.

When the diplomatic expediency of a particular big power favors a misrepresentation of reality, all kinds of old emotional residue are bound to find release, being the very antithesis of the proclaimed loftiness of purpose. In the case of Jewish nationalism, there is the additional danger of long outdated conflicts continuing to condition, by sheer force of tradition, the attitude of the USSR and all those to whom that attitude serves as example.

Freedom from paralyzing chains of tradition is the

very first freedom asserted by revolutionaries, and it is claimed not merely in order to replace unchanging old traditions with unchanging new traditions. There is a choice between habits of thought and the habit of thinking, the former being an apt characterization of the reactionary mind. If yesterday's progressive ideas are not to be frozen into today's reaction, we must make sure that the positions we take are not due to traditions of thought and that they are reached while we perpetually examine ourselves for dogmatic stubbornness. With reference to the Middle East this necessitates that before delineating the regional forces of progress and reaction, we must study them rather than rely on untested assumptions to tell us which is which.

Perpetuity of Rights

If the Arab refugees have not lost title to their lands after nearly two decades, as they most certainly have not, the question arises whether one ever loses title to property of which one is forcefully deprived. The Arabs say that one *never* loses title. If this be so, the historic question arises: when, at what point, did the Jews lose their title to Palestinian territory? When Titus conquered them? When their rebellion and brief independence in the second century A.D. collapsed? When successive foreign rulers up to the recent days of the Turks and the British either prevented or rendered difficult their massive return?

Arnold J. Toynbee, the distinguished British historian, applies a statute of limitations to the Jews' claim to Palestine. But this is a purely arbitrary, if not capricious, adjudication. Certainly, statutes of limitations cannot apply *before* the end of the consequences of a given act. It would be an unjust and cruel statute indeed if it severed due liability without waiting for remedy to take effect. Liability must be as lasting as the injury to which it applies.

Only if Toynbee were right in his view of the Jews as a fossil, would he also be right in applying his statute of limitations. For why maintain liability that can compensate no one? But, whatever one's assessment of today's Jewish culture, the Jews themselves are by no means fossils; they are living human beings, who die when gassed, shot or drowned. And they have all too often in history been gassed, shot or drowned as a result of that forced dispersion to which Toynbee is now willing to apply his statute of limitations. The trouble, and contradiction, obviously emerges from Toynbee's reversed sequence, wherein the liability for a crime lapses before the crime itself is halted.

Farfetched as is this historiological argumentation, it cannot be avoided if the discussion of Israel's very legitimacy is not once and for all considered anachronistic. There is some mixup in sequence when contraception is recommended to prevent a birth that has already occurred. If the Zionist aspiration of creating a Jewish state in Palestine was intolerable, the time to overrule it was before a homogeneous Jewish society had emerged in Palestine. The embryo should not have been allowed to develop. But even later, in the post-World War II years, the international community had an opportunity to overrule the Zionist ambition; it could have prevented the emergence of the State of Israel. But the international community has not prevented this, on the contrary, it has officially voted for the establishment of the Jewish state. Whether its decision was right or wrong, it was irrevocable no less than parenthood is irrevocable. The only option of revocation of parenthood is through infanticide; and a reversal of an international decision permitting the emergence of an independent nation would be its proportionate equivalent: genocide. All who reject this as an alternative, must view any continued discussion of Israel's right to exist as outdated by at least two decades.

Historic rights do have current *moral,* if not proprietary, implications. While they can hardly determine titles to real estate, they can serve as a reminder that the consequences of the exile of the Jews from their ancient land have endured for nineteen hundred years no less tragically than have the consequences of the exile of the Arabs for the past nineteen years. And it is precisely because there is a cause-and-effect chain that ties together the Jews' martyrdom and their loss of homeland that their settlement in Palestine is a *return.*

The institution of nation states may account for many of humanity's past, present and future troubles. But it does exist, at least so far and for the foreseeable future.

Obviously, a decisive number of people are convinced that their nation state affords them some security and protection of interests. Man is thus born not merely with the right to physical locus and air, but also with the right for his locus to be a part of the national organization into which he was born. If this is man's right then it is also the Jewish man's right. In fact, however, Jews had been deprived of this right for nearly two millenia. The duration of this default does not sanctify it.

If a Jew, like anyone else, has a right to be part of his own nation and share in its territory, then the question of which territory is going to be his becomes one of relative rather than absolute merits. If the assumption is that, like any other peoplehood, the Jews, if they so desire, have a right to territorial concentration, then some spot on earth must necessarily be theirs. Then there is no question *whether* they have a right to some territory, but merely *which* territory it is. However one may be inclined to belittle their historic rights to Palestine, certainly, as an ethnic group as well as on the basis of their own cultural values and sentimental attachments, they have a greater link to Palestine than to any other territory on earth. Proof of this lies in the fact that none of the experiments of Jewish colonization other than in Palestine—in Argentina, Crimea, Biro-Bidjan and elsewhere—was successful. If Palestine should be denied the Jews, for reasons of inadequate historic claim, then the Jews can certainly not raise stronger claims toward any other territory. Which is a *reductio ad absurdum* unless the Jews are to be excepted from the universal right to national territory.

The community of nations does have a responsibility toward the Jews for all that has been happening to them, particularly including their decimation only a generation ago. The community of nations cannot adopt the attitude that regrettable as is what has happened to the Jews, it bears no responsibility for finding a solution to their exceptional status, and that even when the Jews themselves do find a solution in the form of wresting for themselves sovereignty, it has no obligation to uphold it. Least of all could the community of nations declare itself neutral toward a political or military process that would now make possible the completion of that genocide which Nazi Germany committed on European Jewry.

If the veterans of all the persecuted peoples, the Jews, had no right to emancipate themselves, then certainly no other, relatively less persecuted, group has that right. Then all revolutions are inadmissible, all anti-imperialist struggles spurious, and the national liberation movements unjustified. Israel is the product of the first of the national liberation movements—one that dates back to before the turn of the century—and its successors cannot be justified without it being justified. The triumph of idealism represented by the emergence of Israel in 1948 has served as an inspiration and source of strength to many peoples of Asia and Africa that have wrested their independence later. Which big power's foreign office finds it now expedient to rewrite history and to tell us that dark forces have alchemically synthesized Israel just so it can be in other peoples' way to freedom?

More important than history are people. Historically right or historically wrong, here they are to be contended with. Unless someone is ready to advocate the mass extermination of people, historic rights, however defined, become undecisive and subordinate to the right to live.

Certainly, there must be something wrong with such an interpretation of the historic tasks of progressive people and the national liberation forces as, in effect, denies the right to life instead of upholding it. The spectacle of communists, socialists and Asian and African anti-imperialists supporting the policies of unreformed pro-Nazi Arab leaders is unbelievable despite its sad reality. No presumed ideological or political consistency is worth such dehumanization. After all, ideological abstractions must be tested by their effect on people. To consider oneself progressive and liberty-minded despite, in effect, supporting policies of mass extermination entails all that moral callousness which a generation ago made possible Jewish extermination in the face of global indifference.

The only objectivity and humanitarianism applicable to the Middle East conflict are those which permit of no obliteration of peoples, Arab or Jewish. It is possible to torture logic until it "proves" anything. At times, there is no obvious demarcation line between the logical discourse and the demagogic discourse. Convincing ideological, political and sociological configurations can be made up in behalf of virtually anything. Our judgment is fallible and even when we judge well, there can hardly be the assurance that all relevant factors have been considered and all irrelevant ones disregarded. But there is one ultimate test of validity; any theory, philosophy, or politics that favors the obliteration of a people is wrong; any theory, philosophy or politics that proceeds from the assumption of everyone's right to live proceeds from the correct assumption. If *this* be arbitrary, "unobjective" or "unscientific," so be it. A thousand historical rights and a million cries of foreign intrusion, even if factually correct, would never add up to anyone's prerogative to eliminate a people, its society and its self-determination.

The main task of objectivity in the Middle East is to insist that the Arabs have no more right to exterminate Israel and the Israelis than the Israelis have to exterminate the Arabs and their states. Without this premise, nothing can be said objectively and no moral equation is valid. The shrewdest argument for one side or the other produces nothing but demagogy if it violates any society's right to exist. And, anything is justified if it is indispensable for upholding that principle. If there is no way to defend it other than through the brutality of war, and if upholding it results in such injustices as a refugee phenomenon, these situations must still be considered as an immensely lesser evil than that of compromising the principle of every ethnic entity's right of survival.

If the Germans, as a nation and as individuals have not lost their right to exist after what they had done to others in World War II, certainly the Israelis have not lost their right to live no matter how many Arab arguments against them might be accepted as valid. A philosophy that, in some kind of argumentative word game, permits the gambling away of nations is neither the philosophy of progress nor the philosophy of humanitarianism; it is clearly, directly and precisely that philosophy on which Nazism rested. No one can adopt it without acquiring a Nazi-like sense of values. Political movements and intellectual communities which embrace it, no matter what their past, and no matter how progressive their origin, succumb to reaction.

What the Nazis did to the Jews was not wrong because of the colors of their uniforms, nor because of any theoretical configurations, but because of the denial of life and everything else; if the same thing is now to be repeated under new colors and sanctified by new word combinations, the deed will, nonetheless be the same morally. It is not *who* commits a crime that determines whether a crime is being committed. What the Germans had no right to do, the Arabs have no right to do, either. And the support of, or indifference to, such deeds is no less immoral when displayed by communists than when displayed by Pius XII. Those progressives who absentmindedly find themselves aligned contrary to their own principles of life and liberty, owe it to themselves to re-examine the peculiar intellectual or other labyrinths through which they arrived at *such* ultimate inconsistency.

Relations Between Neighbors

M. S. Arnoni

Application for Genocide

One thing one cannot deny the Arab leaders: they have been amazingly candid about their desire for war and their resolution to use hoped-for victory for exterminating, hanging, strangling and throwing into the sea the Jews of Israel. But listening to their non-Arab apologists one would never guess that any such morbid candor exists or has ever existed and that any such gory promises are on record. Over the protests of their clients, the apologists are entering a plea of "Not Guilty" in the court of public opinion.

Typically, when this writer was asked to participate in a progressive New York forum on the Middle East, there was not an Arab spokesman he could debate. The suggestion to the forum's organizers that an Arab spokesman be invited was countered with the argument that "Arabs make poor spokesmen for themselves; they don't know how to get their case across to a progressive audience." My interpretation of this as an apprehension that the Arabs' candor about their genocidal ambition would constitute the barrier, remained unchallenged. Not unexpectedly, in the course of the public debate that followed, an American-Jewish "progressive," pragmatic and public relations minded, labored hard to obfuscate what few Arabs would try to obfuscate: the intention to annihilate Israel.

Not only in emotion-charged speeches before their own people but also in well-premeditated statements in the United Nations, Arab leaders continue to insist that the very existence of Israel constitutes aggression. Israeli charges of harassment and sabotage by infiltrators are countered by Arab spokesmen with the claim that since the very emergence of Israel constitutes injustice and aggression, *any* act against her is legitimate self-defense. On June 3, 1967, for example, when the Syrian representative in the Security Council, Abid Doudy, offered a rejoinder to a long list of Israeli charges of assaults, he did not even address himself to the particulars, but instead stated:

> Contrary to what he [the Israeli representative] said, the crisis in the Middle East started, as a matter of fact, on November 29, 1947, when the former President of the United States, Truman, used all the influence and might

of the United States to impose the partition of Palestine . . .

Even in euphemisms the Arabs have been quite uncompromising with regard to their ultimate postulate. The only "humanitarian" version occasionally sounded by their own propagandists, who feel ill at ease in advocating throwing the Israelis into the Mediterranean, is that the Jews go back to the European countries of their origin. Besides the fact that the majority of the Israelis are not European in origin, and that a significant number of them are native born, the very impossibility of the suggestion, not to speak of its hair-raising cruelty, proves it not to be meant seriously but merely as a camouflage of a genocidal intention. It has no more practical merit than the suggestion that all the Americans be sent back to their ancestors' countries of origin.

But usually, Arab talk is even more blunt and threatening than that, and if the Israelis have on many occasions reacted to border raids with an out-of-proportion military intensity, that propensity has been nourished by constantly hearing themselves destined for slaughter. As a reminder of the type of promises they have been exposed to from their neighbors here are a few typical ones.

Robert St. John notes, for example, that during 1959 Nasser repeatedly spoke of "extermination" as his goal *vis-a-vis* Israel.[28] Radio Cairo and the equally controlled Egyptian press have been echoing these sentiments for years. In March 1963, for example, the newspaper *Al-*

---

[28] St. John, *op. cit.,* p. 307.

Gumhuriya published an official announcement which included a metaphor frequently invoked by Arabs when speaking of Israel:

> The noose around Israel's neck is tightening gradually.

No, this is no hyperbole á la Khrushchev's "we will bury you," which was so unfairly exploited in the West. By constrast, the Arab threats are literal, coming within well-structured arguments and being derived from a fixed historical perspective. The Jews in the Middle East are strangers, they don't belong there, they must be removed; and removal in war is usually by death.

Radio Cairo was vowing, on May 25, 1967:

> The Arab people is determined to wipe Israel off the map.

Ahmed Shukairy, the then undisputed leader of Palestinian Arabs and would-be ruler of a conquered Israel, solemnly vowed:

> There will be no Jewish survivors in the Holy War of liberating Palestine.[29]

While Syrian President Nureddin el-Attassi was pledging "total war," his Defense Minister, Hafiz Asad, pledged on May 24, 1967:

> We shall never call for nor accept peace. We shall only accept war and the restoration of the usurped land. We have resolved to drench this land with our blood, to oust you, aggressors, and throw you into the sea for good.

Nasser was repeating his own refrain. In a press conference on May 28, 1967, he ruled out "any possi-

---

[29] Quoted in a "Joint Israeli-Arab Statement on the Middle East Crisis" by the Israeli Socialist Organization and the Palestinian Democratic Front—published by the Bertrand Russell Peace Foundation as an advertisement in the *Times,* London, June 8, 1967.

bility of coexistence with Israel," and in another press conference the following day he said:

> If we have succeeded to restore the situation to what it was before 1965 [by imposing the blockade in the Straits of Tiran], there is no doubt that God will help us and will inspire us to restore the situation to what it was prior to 1948 [when Israel was established].

He must have quickly received confirmation of God's intention, for on June 4, 1967, one day before the outbreak of all-out hostilities, Nasser was saying over Radio Cairo:

> We are facing you in the battle and burning with desire for it to start, in order to obtain revenge.

Egypt's Nasser and Saudi Arabia's Faisal may have their respective supporters, and forces, confronting each other in the Yemen and Aden, but on the issue of Israel both appear to be equally "progressive." In May, the King was in London. Interviewed over the BBC and asked about his policy on Israel, he smilingly defined it, "Extermination of Israel."

Algeria's President, Col. Houari Boumediene, too, was swept away by the mob's cry for blood when, on June 4, 1967, he broadcast this pledge to his people:

> The Arab struggle must lead to the liquidation of Israel . . .

The Soviet Union and other socialist and newly independent countries may pretend never to have heard these statements by the supreme leaders of the Arab world, but this makes these statements no less real. Fidel Castro, who has not yet developed an interest in *preventing* revolutions, even while supporting the Arab position, could not accept revolutionary sanctification of genocide. In an interview he granted K. S. Karol and which was published in the *New Statesman* (London) of September 22, 1967, "He added that he had been shocked, in the period leading to the war, by Arab propaganda of a kind that revealed the lack of revolutionary principles. 'True revolutionaries never threaten a whole country with extermination,' he said. 'We have spoken out clearly against Israel's policy, but we don't deny her right to exist.' "

Comforting as is this verbal disassociation from genocide, it does not obscure the sad fact that nation-murder in the Middle East has not been averted for lack of military, political and diplomatic support from socialist regimes, but *only* thanks to Israel's successful self-defense.

Rejected Alternatives

Not only Israel as now constituted is unacceptable to the Arabs. A smaller Israel was no more acceptable. Typically, in 1955 Major Salah Salem, a member of the Egyptian government, declared:

> Egypt will strive to erase the shame of the Palestine War, even if Israel should fulfil the United Nations resolution; it will not sign a peace treaty with her even if Israel should consist only of Tel Aviv.[30]

Over the decades there have been numerous official and private recommendations for a solution of the Arab-Jewish conflict. They included many partition

30 *Manchester Guardian,* Jan. 28, 1955.

plans, each displaying ingenuity in political and economic geography. There were plans for a federated Palestinian state, with Jewish and Arab sectors. There was a blueprint for confederation. There were suggestions for a bi-national Arab-Jewish state. There were recommendations for a U.N. trusteeship. There was the idea of a Middle East Federation, including Israel. There were designs of every character and there were long, very long, efforts to reconcile any solution with the Arabs. But nothing was ever acceptable short of the liquidation of the Jewish society. This is presented as an unnegotiable Arab objective. As such, it antedates the emergence of Israel as an independent state.

The tragic record shows that the few sane Arab voices, which were willing to consider a solution other than the execution of Israel, have been ruthlessly silenced, or, when physically unreachable by avengers, stigmatized as traitors.

Mere rumors that King Abdullah of Jordan was contemplating a search for some *modus vivendi* for his country's impasse with Israel sufficed to trigger his assassination on July 20, 1951.

Fakhri Abaza, a prominent Egyptian journalist and editor of *El-Mantsur,* had displayed the courage of publishing, in September 1961, an article proposing the formulation of a Middle East Federation that would include Israel. He was dismissed from his editorial position at once.

President Habib Bourguiba of Tunisia has been decried throughout the Arab world as a "traitor to the Arab cause" for the "sin" of suggesting peaceful maneuvers rather than direct belligerence as the method for the Arabs' recovery of all of Palestine.

No one can, of course, *prove* what the Arabs would do if they conquered Israel. We can only surmise this from available indications. Virtually all of them are consistent with total slaughter. Those who believe that all this is no cause for alarm can offer no corroboration. They have nothing better than a subjective intuition to nourish their optimism. Can they—whether they are some government's officials or private individuals—expect Israel to risk its existence on such "guarantees"? Can they expect Israel, on that basis, to remain passive even in the face of any provocation, any act of hostility, any preparations by hostile forces?

Those who do call for such unprecedented "patience" are more likely than not quite willing to accept even the worst fate for Israel.

There are growing signs, however, that a few Arab leaders are beginning to appreciate that they are hurting their own cause by candidly admitting their intentions *vis-a-vis* Israel. King Hussein of Jordan, during a June 1967 visit to the United States, indicated such awareness and his intention to have an Arab summit declare the question to be not Israel's existence but respective Arab-Israeli rights. It is possible therefore that at last talk of exterminating Israel will become less unanimous in the Arab world. But after decades of threats, it will take more than a verbal formula to put at ease all those who insist on Israel's right to live. If the change is merely to be dictated by considerations of propaganda and as such to provide a more convenient international atmosphere in which to prepare for eventual mass murder, then the Arabs will have earned no *quid pro quo*. To be trusted, a change in the official formulation of purpose will have to be accompanied by actual readiness to engage in practical coexistence. It is by such readiness, not by verbal formulations of clever public relations men, that Arab intentions must be judged.

In the aftermath of the June war, the semi-official Cairo daily *Al-Ahram* has, in fact, called for an overhaul of Arab propaganda techniques. This is another reason for skepticism toward any changes thus limited in character. No verbal substitute for coexistence may be legitimized by the international community. Anyone who will help make this clear to the Arab leaders will contribute toward the prospect of averting yet another war in the Middle East.

Between Dialogue and Monologue

Certainly, in situations of contradictory yet in themselves valid claims nothing is more needed than generosity and magnanimity from whomever they might come. At times, what the brain may fail to solve, the heart may be able to cure. It was encouraging therefor to observe, over the years, the proliferation of small groups which hoped to make a contribution to peace through purely humanitarian appeal. They leaned over backward not to impute guilt to the Arab side. As another attraction, they quite deliberately exaggerated whatever criticism they thought Israel to deserve. Even if such things were occasionally done at the expense of truth, the motivation could not have been more commendable.

Unfortunately, none of these efforts in Israel and elsewhere produced anything. Most of the goodwill groups consisted of Israeli or essentially Israeli-oriented intellectuals and students, to whom—if the group had any luck—was added a Gentile professor or two, or a local minister. The only men absent were the most needed ones—Arabs. Some such groups in America may have been so lucky as to have one of their executives duly report that he had had the privilege of clandestinely meeting with an Arab student. The "Arab" may well have turned out to be an Iranian . . . (Whatever exaggeration may be involved in the preceding sentence or two is so slight as, hopefully, to be forgivable.)

The fact is that the Arab world has at no point yet responded to invitations to dialogue. Those who admirably persisted in attempting to arrange it have at times, in the process of cajoling the Arabs, lost their own sense of proportion. They have tried to reflect a balance of a most imbalanced situation. When one is confronted by total hatred and negativism on the one side and by prayers for coexistence on the other, one's stubborn "impartiality" is pathetic. How much acceptance of absolute hatred and how much rejection of appeals for cooperation make the proper formula of a humanism that is not only lofty but also political and effective?

Relative Viability

Much is made of Israel's territory exceeding that envisaged in the original partition plan for Palestine. This is alleged to prove Israel's expansionism. In point of fact, however, Israel, but not the Arabs, had accepted the partition plan. The Arabs, who in 1948 launched a war to prevent the partition of Palestine, cannot suddenly be taken for qualified supervisors of that plan nor for sincere critics of its breaches.

While Arab propaganda has nearly succeeded, by sheer force of repetition, to attach to Israel the stigma of a country that flouts its own birth certificate, the U.N. partition resolution, she alone in her region did not war against that resolution.

But ever since their defeat in 1948, it has been hypocritical for Jordan and Egypt to pose as faithful adherents to the partition plan who may castigate Israel for failing to live up to it. The partition plan envisaged neither Transjordan nor Egypt as successors to the Mandatory regime in any part of Palestine. Transjordan, in conquering lands west of the Jordan River—necessitating a change in its very name—has been in perpetual breach of the partition resolution. Egypt, in occupying the Gaza Strip, has similarly been in breach of the resolution. Besides Israel, there was to be on the territory of the former Mandate, neither Jordan nor Egypt, but a separate Arab state. Even if we, for a moment, set aside the question of both initial and ultimate responsibility for the incomplete compliance with the U.N. partition plan, it is not only Israel's boundaries that are inconsistent with that plan but also those of the UAR and Jordan. Even if we equate the country which accepted the plan with those countries which challenged it, there are three countries in breach of the U.N. decision, not one. For two of them to pose as the public prosecutors of the third is explainable in terms of imposture; for outsiders to accept them in that role is plain stupidity.

Israel's justification for holding some additional territory stems from the very real differences between the vital conditions of a country at peace and those of a country under siege. Israel as envisaged in the partition plan, although in a smaller territory than now, would be a viable state because it would be at peace and because it would be economically united with the rest of Palestine. In addition, its longest border would be shared with another small and peaceful Palestinian state rather than with the much larger and hostile kingdom of Jordan.

But all this did not come to pass. Instead of the envisaged tranquility, Israel, at its birth, had to defend itself against the armies of all her neighbors and not only neighbors. After she had succeeded, she could not relax her security, for the military threat continued right on. Purely demographic considerations, which had served as a base for the Palestine partition, no longer sufficed, for now strategic points acquired life-giving and life-denying importance. With the need for exhausting security budgets and without economic union with the rest of Palestine, the Jewish state's viability became subject to additional conditions.

All these changes in the vital needs of Israel were due to Arab non-cooperation with the partition plan. It is on good moral grounds therefore that the bill for these changes should be paid by those who made them necessary. The Arab world was not offered the partition plan as a minimum to which it could return any time if its military efforts to abort it did not succeed.

The addition of territory to Israel, in 1948, did not occur as a result of a perennial expansionist design, but as a result of a war that was admittedly imposed from the outside. Not the Israelis but the Arabs went to take over the others' territory. That in so doing the Arabs have suffered losses was a risk as fully predictable as it was acceptable to them. Any belated adherence to Israeli borders as envisaged in the partition plan would in effect establish an aggressor's retroactive immunity from loss in combat. It is justified no more than German demands for a restoration of their country's pre-war boundaries. But even this analogy does not suffice, for the Arabs have never yet stated a willingness to co-exist even with a territorially compromised Israel. Thus a more apt analogy would be with Germans who, insisting on their pre-war boundaries, also insist on again trying to destroy their neighbors.

The Soviet Union is, morally, in a particularly untenable position when displaying outrage at the factual change of Israeli boundaries as a result of war. If, as Soviet and other spokesmen do not tire of reiterating, the precedent of boundary changes in war may not be established, no matter what the genesis of the military action, then the Soviet Union herself must give up extensive territories annexed from several nations as a result of World War II.

No more is the Soviet Union justified in championing the Security Council's imposition of sanctions against Israel unless it relinquishes the Old City of Jerusalem. Even before the Old City fell to the Israelis, it was under an administration other than envisaged in the U.N.-adopted partition plan for Palestine. Never once throughout those nineteen years has the Soviet Union recommended sanctions against Jordan to make her relinquish the Old City. What was for nineteen years improper *vis-a-vis* the Jordanians, has overnight become proper *vis-a-vis* the Israelis? But, of course, it would be naive to assume that the USSR is either in the Jordanian or in the Israeli case acting on its sense of justice and legality; it is merely engaging in traditional big power politics, no matter who needs to be hurt in the process.

Suspensibility of Rights

One's right to live does not include one's right to deny life to others. However indisputable are the rights of the Arab refugees, if their exercise is to be lethal to others, the immediacy of their justification is lost. So long as the Arab leaders themselves tell us that their insistence on the repatriation of hundreds of thousands of refugees is intended as a method of blowing up Israel from within, even the invoked right to repatriation is mere camouflage for murder.

Israel would have to suffer from a suicidal complex not to heed the unending barrage of Arab professions of intent of which the two following ones are typical. Said President Nasser on September 1, 1960:

> If the refugees return to Israel, Israel will cease to exist.

And Radio Cairo's Voice of the Arabs stated on September 13, 1961:

> It is obvious that the return of one million Arabs to Palestine will make them the majority of Israel's inhabitants. Then they will be able to impose their will on the Jews and expel them from Palestine.

Even if by Arab standards this latter statement is moderate, Israelis can hardly find in it and its equivalents an incentive for the mass repatriation of the Arab refugees. No doubt, if I had another man's gun and he insisted I return it at once so he can shoot me, I would hardly let myself be impressed by his, in itself justified, claim of ownership.

Much is made of the alleged discrimination against Arab citizens in Israel. The sheer drama of thinking a

Jewish society to be persecuting an ethnic minority in its midst is so diabolically fascinating that a sense of morbid "artistry," if nothing else, may be responsible for the grossest of exaggerations. Then, too, the united racists of the world find in such stories an irresistible vindication of themselves. It is like the CIA hiring Kenyan students to enroll in Moscow University in order at a given time to protest alleged racist discrimination and thus to support American racists with the alibi that "human nature" itself is rotten under *all* political systems.

Any degree of racial, ethnic or religious discrimination is, alas, so totally condemnable that the phenomenon of the oldest victims themselves practicing it is truly preposterous. Yet, if one appreciates that the kernel of truth contained in the cynically exaggerated accusations amounts, in the main, to by now mostly rescinded military restrictions due to the state of war the Arab states insist on maintaining *vis-a-vis* Israel, then even this matter emerges in a different light. We may again be confronted with rights in a state of suspension. The Americans, during World War II, at a distance of thousands of miles of ocean from their Japanese enemy, nonetheless put their citizens of Japanese extraction in administrative camps. Reprehensible as this was and much as it may have been influenced by the deep roots of American racism, it nonetheless was not an exceptional practice among states at war.

The security problem posed to Israel by its Arab

citizens, many of whom are openly hostile and as such identify with the state's enemies just across the so near border, is at least as formidable as was that posed to Czechoslovakia by its Sudeten Germans, who ultimately did dismember the state. Tragic as are situations in which human rights must be weighed as against legitimate considerations of state security, at least in Israel's case there is the slight consolation that it might, just might, be preferable to be nowadays an Arab in Israel than it was a generation ago not only an American of Japanese ancestry, but a Volga German, Crimea Tatar, Kalmyk, or Chechen, Ingush, Karacha or Balkar tribesman in the Soviet Union. Not even the most malicious description of Israel's treatment of its Arab minority begins to approach the treatment the USSR admittedly accorded minorities whose loyalty in war could not be taken for granted.

But even where Arab rights are unequivocal, judgment may be perplexed. While it is true that in the area that became Israel in 1948 only 8.6% of the land was Jewish-owned, contrary to widespread belief, not the major portion but only 20.2% of the land was Arab-owned. (Of that over 3% is owned by Arabs now living in Israel.) The rest, over 70% of the entire land area, had been inherited by the British Mandatory from Turkey whose rule over Palestine ceased in 1918.[31] This governmental land reverted to the State of Israel. It in-

31 *Survey of Palestine,* Government of Palestine, Government Printer, 1946, p. 257.

cludes the Negev area, whose agricultural and industrial development began only under Israeli control.

Historically relevant is also the fact that what is commonly known as "Palestine" is but a small part of the historic land. Israel's boundaries, as determined in the 1949 armistice agreements with her neighbors, gave her less than 18% of the Palestine area of 1922 (8,000 sq. miles out of a total of 45,000). In that year, the British severed from Palestine the major portion of its land (35,000 sq. miles) and, as Transjordan, put it under a separate administration, When, in 1946, it gained independence, a sovereign Arab state in any part of Palestine had been established for the first time in history.

Also relevant is the fact that of the three countries which have, in 1948, taken over what had remained of Palestine—Israel emerging as a state, Transjordan annexing some lands west of the Jordan, and Egypt taking over the Gaza Strip—Israel was the only one empowered by the U.N. partition plan to hold any Palestinian soil.

Yet, none of this diminishes the indisputable merit of the claim that lands left behind by Arab refugees and taken over by the Israelis have, legally, *not* changed ownership.

But the Arabs are mistaken in assuming that the Israelis have no valid counter-claims. These counterclaims are not only those of Jewish refugees who have settled in Israel, leaving their property in the Arab homelands. They derive not from relations with Arabs, but from catalytic factors of the Jews' own history and sociology.

Arab Confessions

Up until the war of June 1967, there was hardly a need to document Arab intransigence; it was indisputable. In view of the Arab's own statements, it was impossible to pretend unawareness of their meaning. The very insistence of the Arabs on maintaining a state of war with Israel and their refusal to either endorse peace as an objective or actually to negotiate sufficed for identifying the aggressors in the Middle East. Of course, with a state of war imposed, formally and/or in fact, there could be no Arab monopoly of belligerence, but whatever Israel did as a result—whether or not it reflected good judgment—was a *response.*

But following Israel's lightning victory over the UAR, Syria and Jordan in June 1967, psychologically, it became immensely easier, if no better founded, to attribute aggressive intent to Israel, not to the Arab states. It appears logical to impute humility to the vanquished and bellicosity to the victor, for why would the weaker party have started a fight? Unfortunately, aggressors have a long history of miscalculating their strength and prospects of success. It is thus not the outcome of a fight, but its origin that determines the aggressor. Otherwise we would have to conclude, for instance, that Nazi Germany was an attacked country in World War II.

To contend, after nearly two decades of Arab insistence, in theory and practice, on a state of war with Israel, that the Israelis, not the Arabs, are the aggressors—is nothing but a replacement of semantics with insanity.

The Arabs themselves confuse the issue of responsibility for aggression only a little. Being neither pragmatists nor public relations-minded people, they are quite candid about themselves and their intentions.

But the Arabs' candor concerning their war intention of May 1967 was matched by their apologists no more than their admissions of the general intent to exterminate Israel. Among the apologists are so many people versed in the ways of international diplomacy that propaganda tactics have been applied to neutralize Arab self-incrimination. Eventually, the propagandists succeeded in confusing issues and in obscuring what had been clear even from the Arabs' own pleas. The indisputable was made disputable.

That is why today there is already a need actually to document Arab intransigence.

Some of the already quoted threats of exterminating Israel were tied specifically to the self-advertised Arab war preparations of May 1967. But there were at the time many additional admissions of aggressive intent, even if not necessarily accompanied by promises of extermination.

While visiting Cairo, shortly before the outbreak of hostilities, Secretary-General U Thant did not need to wonder about the sincerity of anyone's peace professions; there were none. Instead, he heard mobs shouting in the streets, "We want war!" The Syrian President, Dr. Nureddin el-Attassi, who was soon to fly to New York and there to castigate Israel for alleged intransigence, before becoming a loser, did not hesitate to tell his troops on the Israeli border, "We want war with no limits!" Nor did President Nasser hesitate to announce, on May 6, 1967, after amassing an unprecedented force in the Sinai:

> We intend to open a general assault against Israel. This will be total war. Our basic aim is the destruction of Israel.

President Arif of Iraq was ready, too. On June 1, 1967, he called on his compatriots:

> My sons, this day is the day of the battle and of revenge . . . With the help of God we will meet together in Tel Aviv and Haifa.

Nasser told the Central Council of Arab Trade Unions on May 26, 1967, not only that "the Arabs want to fight," but also "that we have been waiting for the suitable day." He had vowed as far back as February 1967:

> It is we who will dictate the time; it is we who will dictate the place [of war with Israel].

In May the time had come, and the place was to be Sharm-el-Sheikh. Nasser himself had said so in addressing the trade union council:

> Sharm-el-Sheikh implies a confrontation with Israel.

The last possible doubt in Nasser's favor, namely that he was merely engaging in demagogic oratory, was dispelled during the post-war Cairo trials of high Egyptian officers. A relevant news item in *The New York Times* of March 3, 1968, stated:

> President Gamal Abdel Nasser . . . is reported to have

> warned his advisers last May that the Egyptian move to block the Gulf of Aqaba to Israeli shipping meant certain war with Israel.
> The disclosure is one of several gleaned from Egyptian radio and press reports of the trials of senior Egyptian military officers in Cairo late last month.

The news item, which was based on "a statement made public by the [UAR] Government" and reported in "delayed Egyptian press accounts," proceeded to disclose that on two fateful occasions Nasser was assured by the late Field Marshal Abdel Hakim Amer, then supreme commander of the Egyptian armed forces, that the military "was ready for war." These assurances were given prior to the expulsion of the U.N. patrols from the border areas and prior to announcing the blockade against Israel in the Gulf of Aqaba.

This was not Nasser and Amer addressing a public rally, but engaged in secret strategic planning. On this level of consultation, there is no bluff—only the real thing.

The Syrians were to provoke the Israelis by increased border infiltration accompanied by boastful public announcements. The Egyptians would come to Syria's "defense" in case of Israeli retaliation. Syrian President el-Attassi himself stated over Radio Damascus on April 17, 1967:

> Anyone who asks for weapons will be given them. Our training centers are open to any Arab citizen. We emphasize that we cannot but stand by the Arab fedayeen, but we are ready for the campaign.

El Chiad, a Lebanese weekly, could report on May

3, 1967:

> Syria will redouble her support of the Palestinian sabotage organization El-Fatah, according to the declaration of a senior Syrian official.

Loud promises of support for Syria in case of an Israeli reaction to her self-advertised border raids, accompanied by ominous troop movements, the eviction of the U.N. Emergency Force, and, finally, the imposition of a blockade in the Gulf of Aqaba were all calculated to provoke Israel into firing the first shot now that Nasser believed the Arab world "completely ready" to "conquer" Israel. Even the miracle of a Nasser-Hussein military pact has now taken place. The midwife of this newest product of loveless immaculate conception was Ahmed Shukairy, leader of the Palestine Liberation Organization. Radio Cairo was confident and arrogant on May 30, 1967:

> Faced by the blockade of the Gulf of Aqaba, Israel has two choices, both of which are drenched with Israel's blood; either it will be strangled by the Arab military and economic siege or it will be killed by the bullets of the Arab armies surrounding it from the south, from the north and from the east.

War was coming in the Middle East. The sole question was how to create the best psychological circumstances for attributing responsibility to the intended victim. Yet, the only ones who seemed unconcerned about the situation and unable to discern danger were the Russians and their allies. In the Security Council—as we have already noted—they just could not understand the "artificial" air of crisis nor the need for emergency meetings . . . Simultaneously, however—as we also have noted—they were feeding the Syrians false reports of Israeli troop concentrations on the border. On June 9, 1967, Nasser said:

> Our friends in the USSR warned the visiting parliamentary delegation in Moscow at the beginning of last month, that there exists a plan of attack against Syria.

That allegations of heavy Israeli concentrations on the border with Syria were without foundation is supported not only by Prime Minister Eshkol's offer to the Soviet ambassador without prior notice to tour any part of Israel, but also by an explicit statement of U.N. Secretary-General U Thant, based on information from his on-the-spot observers. In his report to the Security Council, Mr. Thant declared on May 19, 1967:

> There have been in the past few days persistent reports about troop movements and concentrations, particularly on the Israel side of the Syrian border. . . . Reports from UNTSO [United Nations Truce Supervising Organization] Observers have confirmed the absence of troop concentrations and significant troop movements on both sides of the line.

Soviet Denials

Soon, the Russians had other exclusive "information." It must have caused the Arabs to be apprehensive lest their proud warrior spirit not get its due recognition: contrary to all the Arab governments knew about themselves, the Russians "knew" them to be peace-loving victims of aggression . . .

A month after the fighting, an Arab monarch, King

Hassan II of Morocco, criticized his fellow Arabs for having precipitated a propaganda setback "due to the fact that for seven days the Arab states busied themselves by declaring they were in a state of general mobilization and ready to attack the adversary."[32] But no one "informed" by Soviet diplomats would be apprised of what "the Arab states busied themselves" with for seven days. One would, instead, be led to assume that, as always, they were busying themselves with peace-making, while the Israeli "aggressors," also as always, were threatening to annihilate them.

Soviet leaders have been referring to Israel as "the aggressor" with such mechanical persistence that listening to them one would never guess that there exists anyone in the world taking exception to the Soviet designation. Terminological contraband is relied on to establish the politically loaded synonym of "Israel" and "aggression." To achieve this semantic surgery the international imitators of Madison Avenue remain deliberately oblivious to all controversy and keep repeating their refrain with the air of spokesmen for a unanimous mankind. It is the very same technique which is used by Lyndon Johnson when he labors to make the terms "Ho Chi Minh" and "aggressor" inseparable.

No contradiction, however factual, is allowed to interfere with the droning repetitiousness. True enough, the USSR itself had, on October 18, 1957, proposed in the General Assembly of the United Nations that any

---

[32] *The New York Times,* July 10, 1967.

state first imposing a "naval blockade of the coasts or ports of another State" be "declared an attacker," but why recall this or the fact that the UAR *has* imposed such a blockade, when instead the broken record about Israel's "aggression" can be made to play some more? True enough, both the Syrians and the Egyptians are on record as preparing a war of annihilation, but why take any note of this when instead the broken record can keep revolving? True enough, Israel's attack on a Syrian outpost on April 7, 1967, came in retaliation for a long series of border raids, but why mention that when instead there is yet another Pavlovian opportunity to condition people to associate Israelis and aggressors?

By ignoring the decisive fact that what the state of Israel is forced to defend is its very existence, Soviet leaders try to obscure that they are supporting would-be annihilators of a nation. With Chairman Kosygin and a few other Soviet offiicals paying lip service to the legitimacy of Israel's existence, they can then proceed to offer the Arab governments support without effectively limiting its application. Had Israel been conquered in the last war, by what device would the Soviet Union have made sure that the Arabs would not keep their promise of extermination?

The truth is, of course, that this is not a Soviet worry. Soviet leaders hardly spend sleepless nights worrying about the safety of Israel and the Israelis. The specter of Israel's annihilation is not unconditionally unacceptable to them. At least so far they have not undertaken a single known step to render it impossible or unlikely. On the contrary, by ignoring its seriousness and by unconditionally arming and encouraging those who would wipe Israel off the map, they have utterly divorced their Middle East policy from restraints of conscience.

By no means does all the socialist world hide indifference toward Israel's and the Israelis' survival in propaganda verbiage. On the contrary, there are many who openly profess their opposition to that state's and society's continued existence. An official Chinese statement of June 6, 1967, makes clear that to the Chinese government "Israel is a product of the U.S. and British imperialist policy of aggression." Premier Chou En-lai dispatched, on the same day, a message to Ahmed Shukairy, leader of the Palestine Liberation Organization, pledging China's support for the Palestine Liberation Army. "Your Excellency has on many occasions stated that Palestine can be liberated only by armed struggle," said the Chinese Premier, and added, "I very much admire this clear-cut view held by Your Excellency."

Some of the Cuban-oriented revolutionaries, too, make opposition to the continued existence of Israel a cardinal premise. Even before the Arab-Israeli war of June 1967, the First Tri-Continental Conference of Solidarity of the Peoples of Africa, Asia and Latin America, held in Havana between January 3 and 12, 1966, condemned in its resolution on Palestine "the existence of Israel in the occupied territory of Palestine," recognized the "right of Palestine to free itself" and stated that it "FIRMLY SUPPORTS the Palestine Liberation Organization . . ." (Caps retained.)

Soviet spokesmen deny supporting genocide and claim their policy to be progressive, *because* it *acknowledges* Israel's right to exist; the Chinese and others claim their policy to be progressive *because* it *denies* Israel the right to exist. Logic seems to demand that these two positions be considered in direct conflict with one another. In fact, however, they are considered on the Left to vary only in degree, not in essence. There is realism in this denial of essential difference, for in effect, if not in verbiage, the Soviet indifference to Israel's survival, as a state, society and even as individual men, is as total as that of those who profess it openly.

Ideologically, however, the difference is of consequence, for it confuses the whole progressive stereotype of the anti-Israeli position. Is the defense of Israel's survival an indispensable tenet of the progressive position on the Middle East, or does the progressive position sanctify the extermination of Israel? And if the latter, have we not come to absorb within a philosophical framework that fancies itself to be progressive and humane, the Nazi propensity for exterminating whole societies?

Even on the purely theoretical level there is an inconsistency involved in *pro forma* Soviet acknowledgments of Israel's right to exist. More emphatic than these acknowledgments are Soviet professions of implacable hostility toward Zionism. This hostility begets attributions of horrors in which malice is superseded only by fantasy. Yet, Israel *is* the product of Zionism, its self-fulfilment. If the historic Soviet attitude toward the Jewish problem had prevailed, there would have been neither Zionism nor Israel. Why, then, should now equivocal assurances about Israel's right to survive be taken on face value when coming from people, Soviet and other, who, with the exception of a brief post-war period, had devoted a life-time to precluding Israel's very existence? When such men lecture Israel on her vital interests and safest policies, how much Israeli trust can they expect to elicit? Why should lifelong ill-wishers be accepted as friendly counsellors, into whose hands may be entrusted one's very life?

Of all the socialist governments only that of Rumania has dared to engage in some questioning rather than blindly following the Soviet lead. It certainly is no coincidence that that country's leaders, who have displayed integrity in their relationship with China, are now displaying the same virtue with regard to the Middle East. It is precisely because men like Nicolae Ceausescu, the General Secretary of the Rumanian Communist Party, and Premier Ion Gheorghe Maurer insist on adhering to revolutionary morality and refuse to replace it with a devotion to contrary institutional interests of the Soviet apparatus, that the former included in his important speech of July 24, 1967, these morally refreshing words:

> We wish honestly to tell our Arab friends that we do not understand and do not share the position of those circles which speak in favor of the liquidation of the state of Israel. We do not wish to give advice to anybody, but the lessons of history show that no people can achieve their national and social aspirations against the right to existence of another people.[33]

In uttering this reminder at a time when the diplomatic and propaganda machines of all other socialist countries are providing unquestioning all-out support for the Arabs, Mr. Ceausescu has contributed to socialist morality much more than to Israel's cause. Indeed, he emerges as the sole guardian of ideals, while the others are satisfied to serve as the superintendents of the temple's grounds. If ideological consistency is a socialist's concern, he may have it by accepting, on this issue, the position of his Rumanian comrades rather than by submitting to an institutional discipline imposed from Moscow.

The Arabs do deserve to be taken seriously, and not to be treated by their friends and supporters like incoherent little children or madmen. The record of their professions, admissions and deeds must be taken note of. Perhaps the ultimate insult directed at the Arabs comes from their international backers who find it necessary to pretend that that record either does not exist or if it does, does not count.

---

[33] *The New York Times,* July 25, 1967.

The Politics of "Humanitarianism"

M. S. Arnoni

Standards of Judgment

In the aftermath of every war the need for humanism and generosity exceeds their availability. There are more wounds than can be cured, more suffering than can be alleviated, and more victims than can be rehabilitated.

War is, of course, a series of atrocities. That is why anyone imputing atrocities to any belligerent is right by definition. Partisans who report only one side's atrocities need not lie to be wrong, for no participant in mass murder—which war, of course, is—behaves pacifically. Since all belligerents maim and kill, each can justly accuse the other of atrocities and do so with an unjustified air of moral superiority. Even the Spanish fascists could, and did, accuse the loyalists of atrocities, and not all the accusations need have been unfounded. The Nazis could accuse their challengers. They could even accuse the heroic rebels of the Warsaw Ghetto of shooting, burning and killing people.

That all warring is atrocious does not mean, however, that all belligerents stoop to equally reprehensible levels of inhumanity. But if reporting of war atrocities is to be objective, it must not distort the *relative* standards of the respective belligerents. Both sides, for instance, use fire power. If one side confines it to military targets while the other uses it also against non-combatants, then the latter exceeds the former in atrociousness. A war description that would not take note of this, even if distorted in no other way, would be unobjective.

Humanitarian sensitivities can easily be misguided by the sad, if inescapable, relationship between the vanquished and the victor. In war, neither side is a voluntary loser. Hence, the state of being the defeated is no measure of superior morality or stronger scruples. The subdued is not necessarily an angel, and the one who subdued him is not necessarily a villain. Fights are not rigged in a way that would cause the less moral antagonist to succumb. Standing over a man who has been killed one must ask oneself whether his killer might have been killed instead; only if the answer is negative is an innocent victim before us.

Allocating human compassion is one thing, and determining responsibility quite another. That which invokes compassion is not necessarily a guide for determining justice.

Of course, a victor's magnanimity should be taken for granted. Of course, when people suffer, they deserve assistance no matter how and why they had been made to suffer. That is why sympathy for Arab refugees and other war victims is not only justified but an elementary challenge to the Israelis. More than anyone else the Israelis have an obligation to be humanitarian toward the people they defeated. But between this and the misuse of humanitarian appeal for political purposes, and especially for false attribution of war responsibility, there is a big difference. Humanitarian notions are certainly no less—perhaps they are more—necessary than objective adjudications, but the former cannot be accepted as the latter. However great Arab suffering, however regrettable, and however compelling it is to remove it, the responsibility for bringing it about is clearly Arab.

Objectivity can be a rather perplexing challenge. Some people have a purely symptomatic or visual perception of it. They know in advance all too much what must be the characteristics of a judgment that is objectively arrived at. To them, objectivity is the middle point between opponents. But where is the middle point between a moving object and an immobile object? If the latter's motion is only towards the former, soon distance between them will disappear and with it the middle point. All three will then become one, located precisely where the immobile object was to begin with.

This has been happening with some people who think that objectivity requires them necessarily to disassociate themselves from the positions of either partisan to a dispute. When you have an implacable, absolutist and total position, as the Arabs are taking by insisting on Israel's extermination, and the other party's position of seeking compromise and reconciliation, as Israel's position has been over the years, then any middle-of-the-road objectivity is bound to come progressively closer to the former. Soon, it is likely to become indistinguishable from the rigid partisan's position. Now the circle is complete, what with the whole inquiry having begun with a determination to identify with neither of the partisans.

True objectivity, of course, has nothing to do with such mental gymnastics. If one is to judge any given situation in full intellectual freedom—which is probably as good a definition of objectivity as any—then one must claim the full liberty of reaching *any* conclusion, specifically including such as might coincide with either of the partisans in conflict. Without this, what results is not objective judgment but constipated judgment, a judicial function that is hamstrung in advance. Such is prejudice, not objectivity.

Prejudicial as are these *non sequiturs*, one can discern their influence in much of the criticism showered at Israel. For where is the middle point between genocide and reconciliation? How can one place oneself anywhere in between these postulates, much less in the precise middle? There is no such in-between other than in false judges' imaginations. One cannot be *a little* against genocide; one can only be for or against it. Hence that any response to the Arab-claimed right to exterminate Israel other than an absolutely negative response, at least in effect, sanctions the Arab postulate.

If the would-be judge with pretentions to objectivity also happens to be Jewish, then the demonstrativeness of his pretentions to objectivity may produce especially pathetic results. For then at least some rejection of Israeli merits may be undertaken without any reference to the real issues but merely in order to manifest that one has transcended chauvinistic loyalty. One such commentator, while reviewing the June 1967 special issue of Sartre's *Les Temps Modernes* on the Israeli-Arab conflict, actually justified, in so many words, his essentially, if newly-arrived-at, pro-Arab position by the need to do so "as a Jew, closely bound emotionally with the birth of Israel." With a few strokes on a typewriter keyboard, the fate of a whole nation suddenly became dependent on nothing but one man's need to apologize for his birth and to stage a display of the transcended quality of his mind. Well, some troubled people take a walk, others seek out psychiatrists, and still others start rearranging nations. While occasionally such people may succeed in exempting themselves from the travel ban imposed on their co-religionists by the Arab countries, they distort the very meaning of objectivity so completely as to render themselves totally incapable of it.

If a Jew, in order to prove his objectivity, *must* take an anti-Israeli and pro-Arab position, then, by the same logic, an Arab, to prove his objectivity, *must* be anti-Arab and pro-Israeli. While this would be an interesting exercise in intellectual transcendentalism, not much would change politically, for confronting each other would still be two hostile camps, even if with reversed personnel. But, come to think of it, to prove once more the flexibility of their minds, the two parties would again have to reverse their respective positions each recapturing its original point of view. A dizzying *perpetuum mobile* might result, the Middle East becoming entangled in some kind of a political rumba. While one can clearly see how this could save psychiatric fees, it is less certain that it would also cure the region's ills.

Then there are the inverse racists. Understandable alienation from their exploitative and imperialistic Western societies causes them to use a color line of their own as a guide in international relations. Imperialism being to them white, any non-white movement is *ipso facto* right. As for any contest between whites and non-whites, the former are presumed to be playing some imperialist trick as a matter of course, and the latter are presumed to be playing a progressive role as a matter of destiny.

The inverse racism involved is anthropologically quite

flexible. Its criteria are not tied to biological characteristics as much as to attire and outward symbols. To the degree that it afflicts anti-imperialist elements within the imperialist nations, it is spurred on by ignorance of the perplexity and diversity of Eastern cultures. The keffiyeh or turban is taken as a testimonial of social advancement. Granted, there may be exotic charisma in such progressivism but there is a sad dearth of progress in such exoticism.

Yet the new symbols of presumed progress offer welcome relief from old symbols of which, in an era of swiftly passing fashions, one has long since grown bored. With people who would accept something new that is wrong rather than anything old that is right, there attaches a tiresone old-fashionedness to continued sympathy for the long-persecuted Jew. One is relieved of its boredom at the sight of a keffiyeh—promising new excitement of the unknown and perhaps a world less rotten than one's own.

But even within this unsupportable frame of reference it is absurd to categorize the Jews with the persecuting races, the subjugators of the Orient. Least of all have they been conquerors of nations.

Nor is the prejudicial imagery borne out by the Jewish colonizers of Palestine in recent decades. They share nothing with imperialist colons. They did not establish themselves as politically-favored *latifundistas;* they came to be workers and peasants. They did not become absentee landowners, but offered their muscle on the labor market. They did not form an imported make-shift aristocracy, but a social grassroot. They did not relegate "natives" to disdained functions and inferior status, but came to share with them all strata of work and society. They could not differ more totally from the colon image which so correctly stands for imperialist subjugation.

Progressivism-by-keffiyeh and imperialism-by-the-Jew's-Occidentalism may be yet another passing branch of entertainment, but it hardly qualifies as a discipline successor to political science. While the keffiyeh is "in" and the yarmulke is "out," one wonders how soon the former might be replaced by the Rosary. With the status of Jerusalem in dispute, and with some atheists championing the Vatican's cause, the new fashion may be just around the corner.

Much of mankind is perhaps historically conditioned to associate Jews with tragedy, persecution and extermination, and therefore another Jewish tragedy may be psychologically more acceptable than the reality of a fiercely fighting, and successful, Jewish military. If the Arabs won, well, we could all have bleeding humanitarian hearts, again wailing for massacred Jews. But with the Israeli Jews cheating us out of almost nostalgic and humanitarian ego-restoring opportunities, some people may, nonetheless, squeeze out their humanistic self-confirmation from an intellectual overhaul. As the victim of assault stands erect over his subdued assailant, the very least a semi-professional humanitarian can do is wail for the would-be murderer's every scratch. Alas, what kind of humanitarian notion is it that at the end of each battle makes one regret that the winners are not the losers?

Dayan The Terrible

The personality of a particular official of any nation can have no bearing on its right to exist. But nations can, at least to some extent, be judged by the leaders they choose and follow. That is why propaganda machines so often, fairly or unfairly, concentrate on denigrating the leaders of a nation adversary. But common as it may be to hate the leaders of a hated country, the admonishment not to slander and libel people applies precisely when there arises an emotional temptation to do so. Because a great deal of personal slander and libel were resorted to as propaganda weapons against Israel, at least one Israeli personality needs to be discussed here as a case study in the fairness of some anti-Israeli argumentation.

We are talking about General Moshe Dayan, Israel's Defense Minister, who for some reason (other than provided by himself, as we will see) has been made the most maligned man by the Left. Both Soviet and neo-Nazi publications have been depicting him as a spiritual successor to Hitler. Communist newspapers have been falsely presenting him as an "ex-trainer of the Green Berets in Vietnam." (*The Canadian Tribune,* Toronto.) Others credited him with doing "his bit for imperialism by offering his advice on how the U.S. could best reach its goals" in Vietnam, after he had used a period of retirement from governmental service to spend, in 1966, five weeks in Vietnam as a newspaper correspondent. Indeed, Dayan did offer advice even if of a kind quite different from that implied by his character assassins.

Dayan devoted great portions of his Vietnam correspondences to trying to convince the Americans about the futility of their war. Which was not all he had to say to and about them. He described in great detail the corruption and demoralization the Americans are bringing to Vietnam, in addition to reporting that they are warring not merely against a military and semi-military enemy, but against the Vietnamese people at large. The over-all portrait of the U.S. military in Vietnam emerges in a most unfavorable light in any but the technological respect. They are characterized as war-loving, aggressive and contemptuous of the rest of the world. Dayan explicitly speaks of their nationalistic superiority complex. He presents them as foreign intruders and oppressors genuinely hated by the population at large. The Saigon regime backed by the Americans emerges as utterly corrupt, unprincipled and one ruling by terror. He calls its legislative elections "fraud." So damaging is the general picture of the Americans in South Vietnam that American newspapers which had obtained reproduction rights of Dayan's August 1966 correspondences censored out particularly unfavorable parts that did appear in the Israeli press.

But Dayan also had advice for the "Vietcong." In hundreds, perhaps thousands, of words he gave *them* obviously sincere military advice, urging, and urging again and again, that they avoid big-unit frontal confrontations with the Americans, whose fire power they could not possibly match. While he saw no prospect for the liberation forces (yes, of areas under N.L.F. administration, Dayan, as the Vietnamese themselves, speaks as " liberated" areas!) to defeat the Americans, he implores them to rely primarily on guerrilla warfare and everything will turn out just fine at least in preventing an American victory and stabilized hegemony. He describes the "Vietcong" as idealists and dedicated patriots. He speaks of their social reforms, genuine dedication to the people and incorruptibility with unmitigated and candid admiration. He is in outright awe of the heroism of captured guerrilla fighters he encountered.

All this, coming from a former commanding officer of a country to which the National Liberation Front and North Vietnam have been openly hostile, adds up to quite a depth of integrity. That Dayan accepted the hospitality of the U.S. military in Vietnam in the first place was a reason for our own contempt (an initial draft of this review, written before further research was undertaken, contained the sentence, "We have nothing but contempt for Dayan's acceptance of hospitality from the U.S. military in South Vietnam"), until it turned out that the one-sidedness involved was anything but of his own making. In fact, Dayan seems to have hoped to be a "guest" also of the "Vietcong," joining them on their jungle forrays, as he had joined the Americans on theirs. He went to Rangoon, met there with the North Vietnamese consul and asked for permission to visit North Vietnam. He was turned down on the grounds that the North Vietnamese leaders were too busy conducting the war and that his personal safety could not be guaranteed.

Dayan's defense policy may be right or wrong, but neither makes true that which is not true about him. His "activism" may or may not be justified, but to portray this collective farmer and disciple of Israel's Gandhi, A. D. Gordon, as a fascist and militarist *par excellence* involves as little truth as the description of theocratic one-time Nazi collaborator Gamal Abdel Nasser as a progressive and revolutionary leader. In libel and audacity it is second only to Walter Ulbricht's assertion that "Hitler General Rommel is declared the teacher of the Israeli army of aggression." (From a speech delivered in Leipzig on June 15, 1967.)

With all the recent German preoccupation with genealogy, perhaps Herr Ulbricht should have been more discreet about uncovering Rommel's . . . Jewish links. But since he has publicized them, and this on the basis of a not further identified declaration, presumably by the "Israeli army of aggression" itself, if it should turn out that the Israeli army does not acknowledge itself as an "army of aggression" and/or that it does not acknowledge Rommel as its teacher, in such a case, with all due respect for a progressive head of a progressive state, Herr Ulbricht, too, would emerge as a liar. He *does* so emerge.

Napalm

Judicial criteria can easily be lost sight of by witnesses to human suffering. Even without the interference of political motives, the very sadness of what they see may interfere with responsible judgment. But when political motives *are* present, there is almost no possibility for humanitarian sensitivities to retain integrity. An Egyptian doctor, for example, sadly describing his napalm-burned patients, may easily believe himself to be responding to nothing but human suffering, but in actuality his emotions may be greatly influenced by the political Who's Who in the war.

Let us assume, for example and for the sake of clear judgment, that Israel's use of napalm against Egypt's non-use of napalm was due to some Israeli military initiative that neutralized Egypt's supply. We do not know such in fact to have been the case, but assuming that it was, was Israel more ruthless than the UAR? No, for in such a case neither side abstained *voluntarily* from using napalm.

The resort to napalm causes particularly tragic associations, which can easily be exploited not for humanitarian but for political and propaganda purposes. These associations are due primarily to the use of napalm by Americans against the Vietnamese population at large. It is this indiscriminate use rather than the technical aspect of the horrible weapon alone that accounts for its being singled out for special condemnation by so much of mankind. But when used against a tank, for example, napalm produces precisely the same effect as a properly planted Molotov cocktail—it ignites the fuel, causing fire and explosion. The death of the trapped personnel is in either case by fire. However horrifying, purely military use of napalm is consistent with that type of atrocity, which, known as "war," has long since been conventional. It must under no circumstances be confused with the even more outrageous mass murder of civilians.

Least of all do we approve of its use. Napalm is a weapon which both broadens and deepens human suffering beyond that inflicted by many other uses of fire for murder. Yet, war technology has an uninterrupted history of increasing the effectiveness of murder tools. Probably the worst feature of napalm is that wherever applied, there is no further discrimination possible as to its victims. Here again we are back to the decisive aspect of target choosing, and the relative morality of its use—to the degree to which it is possible to speak of any morality of fighting—depends on external specifics rather than on innate nature.

To be sure, the increased damage by fire and the lessened control of application which napalm represents more than suffice to outlaw its use the way dum dum bullets and poison gases have been outlawed. So long, however, as napalm is not internationally outlawed, and so long as not a single government in the world has bindingly committed itself to refrain from ever using it, it would be naive to expect that any army would ban it from its arsenals or hesitate to resort to it when required by military expediency. Thus the sole criterion we are left with, at least for the time being, for judging the propriety of using napalm is one that makes our judgment depend on the target rather than on the fact of application.

While it is likely that the instant air supremacy which Israel had gained over her Arab antagonists prevented the Arabs' own massive use of napalm, there are some indications and sad examples available as to what the Israelis might have expected had they not gained a decisive upper hand. Specifically, as far as napalm is concerned, the *Jerusalem Post* of June 6, 1967, reported that it had been dropped on Kibutz Ein Hamifratz near Haifa. That there were no casualties was due to the availability of shelters, not to Egyptian scruples. Alas, the target under attack was *civilian*—the type of target against which the Americans are applying napalm in Vietnam, causing them justly to be counted among the most brutal and dirty warriors in history.

But we need not base our assumptions as to potential Arab means of warfare on a single event or two. The Egyptians proved quite willing to use poison gas against their own fellow Arabs in the Yemen. The many reports of such attacks having at last been confirmed by the International Red Cross (which the Egyptians had for a long time kept from conducting on-site investigations—even by bombing an investigation team—and which had for a long time given them the benefit of every reasonable doubt),[34] provide an indication of what the Israelis would be exposed to if only the Egyptians had gained a free choice of initiatives.

Nor do we need to speculate about the fate of Israelis under Jordanian occupation. The Israeli army, after occupying Jordan's west bank, has released top secret orders captured in all seven brigade headquarters that fell to it. All contained specific instructions about killing captured civilian Israelis. (The extreme skepticism with which one should receive a belligerent's claims about captured enemy documents does not apply, in equal measure, when the enemy's *professed* goal *is* extermination.) One of the typical orders was that issued by H. Q. IMAM ALY BEN TALEB Brigade (Operations), Registration No.: A'1/1/1 of 7th June 1966 to the Commander Reserve Battalion 27th Brigade. It was captured at the Ramallah headquarters. It amounted to an assignment to destroy the Israeli village Motza near Jerusalem. The instructions were very detailed indeed. Under section "1. Situation" part "B. Own Forces" one reads:

> 1) The intention of H.Q. Western Front is to carry out a raid on MOTZA Colony, to destroy it and to kill all its inhabitants.

Under section "2. The Task" it is further ordered:

> The Brigade Reserve Battalion will raid MOTZA Colony,

[34] *The New York Times,* July 28, 1967.

> will destroy it and will kill all persons in it upon receiving the codeword "*HADHAD*" from brigade H.Q.

Such was to be the fate of the 800 inhabitants of Motza. Such was to be the fate of many, all, Israeli cities, towns and villages under Arab conquest.

Prisoners of War

An example of humanitarian concern being used, deliberately or unconsciously, for political ends was provided by reports that Israel was causing "tens of thousands of Egyptian soldiers to perish in the Sinai Desert without water or treatment of their wounds."[35] This charge by an Egyptian diplomat, Dr. Hussein Khallaf, was echoed internationally and provided, substantially, the basis for "leading Soviet newspapers" to accuse "Israeli troops of genocide against Arab soldiers and inhabitants of border areas seized last week."[36] Soviet officials have voiced similar charges even from the forums of the United Nations. The forcefulness with which these accusations were made actually intimidated many people into criticizing Israel, although no immediate verification was available, lest they have imputed to themselves an indifference to atrocities.

Ironically, it turned out that the indifference to the suffering of the Egyptian soldiers in the desert was less Israel's than Egypt's, which had turned off the water supply in the desert pipeline. Dr. Khallaf's hypocrisy

---

[35] *Ibid.*, June 16, 1967.
[36] *Ibid.*, June 17, 1967.

is fully shown up in the very same news item that reported his complaint:

> Asked to explain why Egyptian authorities had cut off the supply of water in the pipeline under the Suez Canal, which could have provided water for the Sinai area, and had not restored it until two days ago, Dr. Khallaf replied that in any case the pipeline could not provide enough water for more than "one or two hundred" soldiers.[37]

The full cynicism of the accusation is made clear when one realizes that by contrast to Egypt's own callousness Israel *did* make extensive efforts to rescue the stranded Egyptian soldiers. Together with the Egyptian diplomat's accusation, the relevant news dispatch from Geneva included this information:

> The International [Red Cross] Committee explained that its agreement with Israel provided for "the rapid settlement of the humanitarian problems created by the fate of the Egyptian soldiers in the Sinai area."
> It previously reported that Israeli commanders had ordered their forces to give "all possible assistance" to wounded Egyptian soldiers and those who had laid down their arms.[38]

One day later an assessment of the effectiveness of the Israeli efforts was offered in another news dispatch from Geneva:

> All the Egyptian troops still straggling in the Sinai desert are expected to be gathered up and given food and water within hours, the International Committee of the Red Cross said this afternoon. . . .
> The delegates [of the International Committee] are participating in the Israeli Army's efforts to collect, feed and treat the Egyptian stragglers. The Israelis are using planes,

---

37 *Ibid.*, June 16, 1967.
38 *Ibid.*

> helicopters and trucks, the Red Cross said. . . . There was an offer of American help, he [a spokesman] said, but the Red Cross delegates on the spot "seem to have been relying entirely on Israeli communications and transport."[39]

No doubt Arab prisoners of war and those who escaped capture have suffered greatly. Given the reality of war, much of that suffering was unpreventable. But, no doubt, there was also suffering that could have been prevented even in the reality of war. There is some consolation, however, in the following report by an Egyptian physician, Dr. Mohamed Salah, who received thousands of prisoners from the hands of the Israelis:

> To my knowledge, all the men I saw going past and embarking—which was about 4,500 in 36 hours—were treated by the Israelis in accordance with the Geneva Conventions. I heard no complaints of bad treatment.[40]

The Egyptians, in turn, had taken but very few Israeli prisoners. Among those few was a pilot who bailed out when his aircraft was hit. Reuter's Cairo dispatch of June 6, 1967, revealing the prisoner's fate deserves to be quoted in full:

> An Egyptian mob axed an Iraeli pilot to death after he threatened them with a pistol, the newspaper Al Ahram reported here today.
>
> The newspaper said that the pilot had bailed out over Zagazig in lower Egypt and was surrounded by peasants.
>
> The newspaper published a photograph of the pilot, which showed him with head and face wounds. The pilot was not named.
>
> In the photograph, villagers held up the pilot's clothing.[41]

---

39 *Ibid.,* June 17, 1967.
40 *Ibid.,* June 16, 1967.
41 *Ibid.,* June 7, 1967, Reuters.

As if this Egyptian admission of cruelty—which has a Syrian counterpart in the similar fate of another Israeli pilot—needed Israeli confirmation, a diary of Dr. Amnon Rubinstein, a senior law lecturer at the Hebrew University and a mobilized reserve lieutenant in the Israeli Army, provides it:

> That day we took about 700 prisoners of war. They came down from the hills, barefoot, dirty, exhausted. In the daytime they were helpless, harmless. But after sunset, the stragglers could become dangerous. The night before, three Israelis guarding their stranded tank had been attacked and murdered by Egyptian soldiers. Their mutilated bodies, the male organs cut off and placed in their mouths, were found beside the tank. Some of the men were thirsting for revenge. I had to talk to them, to calm them down. Our ways are different from those of the enemy, I told them. The order against mistreating prisoners of war in any manner would be rigorously enforced.[42]

No doubt, it requires less effort and time to concoct false charges than it requires to prove them what they are. Since in cases involving possible cruelty every benefit of the doubt is quite naturally given the accuser, intended political damage may be inflicted without, or despite, evidence. Relevant is one disinterested observer's comment:

> Stories coming out of Arab capitals about atrocities in Israel-conquered territories bear little resemblance to what one finds on the west bank. There are probably two main reasons for the discrepancies. The first is that those who fled have an interest in justifying their fleeing and in stoking up hatred of the Jews, while those who remain want to protect their interests and security.[43]

42 *The New York Times Magazine,* July 2, 1967.
43 Colin Legum, *The Observer,* London, June 25, 1967.

None of this is to say that the Arab military forces are mere savages and their Israeli counterparts etiquette-abiding gentlemen. There has not yet been a humane army at war, and the Israeli has not won the distinction of being the first one. But, again, it is to say that war always involves such atrocities as enable each of the participants to claim, justly or not, moral superiority. In the aftermath of their military defeat, the Arabs are, quite naturally, making the most of their psychological advantage.

As against the barrage of tendentious war reports, one observer offered a picture that is striking for its factual objectivity and historic perspective:

> The astonishing thing about Israel at present . . . is not that there may have been cases of looting by Israeli soldiers or that refugees from the West Bank of the Jordan may have been encouraged to board the bus for the Allenby Bridge. Still less is the universal determination to keep Jerusalem or the refusal to withdraw from the occupied territories until the Arab States make peace. The astonishing thing is the almost total absence of the desire for revenge which most Frenchmen felt about Germany in 1918 and many Englishmen felt in 1945—and which, for that matter, most Arabs have been taught to feel about Israel ever since 1948.[44]

Nor does the paradox of victors suing for peace yet being decried as incorrigible militaristic conquerors escape that observer:

> The idea that the Israelis are anxious to lord it over conquered territories and dictate a Carthaginian peace is ludicrously wide off the mark. They are bemused by victory,

[44] David Marquand, *Manchester Guardian* (Weekly), June 13, 1967.

> not drunk with it. For 20 years they have lived with a knife at their throats. Now the knife has miraculously been removed; and all they want is to make sure that it never returns. Not surprisingly, they are not sure how to do this; and in any case, they cannot do it by themselves. But the will, at least, is there. The world would be a different place if the same will had been present in most victorious countries after most wars.[45]

To resist political manipulation through the good offices of—in themselves justified—humanitarian sympathies one merely needs to imagine the fate of the Israelis if they turned out to be the vanquished. But they would not complain—they would not be likely to be around to do so.

The Other Refugees

Another area in which political motive may hide behind expressed humanitarian concern is that dealing with war refugees. During and following the 1967 Middle East war there was a deluge of reports that the Israeli troops were forcibly evicting Arabs from their towns and villages and chasing them across the border. There have been, however, authoritative reports denying this. Among those coming from Jordan was this item:

> At no time during a number of long talks with Arabs in this area was anything said to support Arab charges at the United Nations that thousands had been forced to cross the Jordan River from the west bank area occupied by the Iraelis.[46]

Another reporter in Amman confirmed that denial:

---

45 *Ibid.*
46 Sydney Gruson, *The New York Times,* June 15, 1967.

> The refugees said that they had not been driven out but that the Israelis had merely let it be known that buses were available to take them to the bridge.[47]

A humanitarian, or public relations, undertaking of the Israelis of providing buses for Arabs wishing to join their families or preferring for other reasons to cross the Jordan was used to impute the opposite type of behavior to them. That such, in fact, was the case was confirmed by an independent source:

> The present daily efflux is being handled in cooperation by Arab municipal councils and the Israelis. It started on June 9 when the former governor of the Old City, Anwar El Khatib, approached the Israeli governor of the west bank, General Chaim Herzog, with a request "on grounds of compassion" to allow those wishing to leave to do so. He claimed that hundreds of children from Jordan's east bank were studying on the west bank, that many of the officials were from Amman, and that others had their families living there.
>
> General Herzog agreed to meet this request and offered free transport for two hours every day to the crossing point at Allenby Bridge. Those wishing to leave are allowed whatever they can manage to get loaded, with no questions asked.[48]

To these one should add another category of refugees fleeing from the Israel-occupied territory:

> The numbers applying to go at first puzzled the Israelis until the important fact was brought to light that a large number of former Palestinian refugees are living on remittances from their relations who work in Kuwait, Saudi Arabia and along the Persian Gulf. About 100,000 Palestinians appear to be employed in the gulf area. . . . Because of fears that these remittances will not reach

---

[47] Dana Adams Schmidt in *The New York Times,* June 17, 1967.
[48] Colin Legum, *The Observer, op. cit.*

> them their families are choosing to go to Jordan. These facts are confirmed by a number of mayors to whom I talked, as well as by United Nations officials and the heads of the old-established Palestine refugee camps.[49]

Yet, we are not critical of those who would rather take a risk of negatively reflecting on an innocent country than of failing to act on the plight of people. Exaggeration, deliberate or inadvertent, in some reports may have in fact put the Israelis on their toes and made a preventive impact. Which was all to the good.

But there have also been reports of other war refugees and somehow their plight has not alerted many of the hearts that had proved so humanitarian while watching the Allenby Bridge over the Jordan River. These were the jailed, pogromed and terrorized Jews of Egypt, Morocco and the other Arab countries. Not one socialist stood up for them in the United Nations. Soviet diplomats were all too busy championing the cause of churches and clergymen in Jerusalem to notice the plight of *these* refugees. Many private individuals, who quite properly would not dismiss a rumor of mistreatment by the Israelis even if coming from an obviously ill-disposed source, showed no concern for the Arabs' captives. They were either swept up by a deafening propaganda barrage, or political motives caused them to unequally apply standards of humanity.

That there was, and continues to be, cause for alarm is beyond doubt. From Geneva came this report:

> An American Jewish leader said today that 600 Jewish

---

[49] *Ibid.*

> men, including Grand Rabbi Jacques Nefoussi of Cairo, were being held in Egyptian jails as a result of the war between Israel and the Arabs. . . . He said that most of the imprisoned Jews, although born in Egypt, were stateless and hence had no government to intervene in their behalf.
>
> Jews born in Egypt must go through a difficult naturalization procedure if they wish to obtain citizenship. There are cases in which a family of Jews that has lived in Egypt for several generations has failed to acquire citizenship.
>
> . . . Most Jews taken into custody have been beaten up, he said, and some have reported broken fingers and other injuries. . . . In Morocco, Mr. Schuster [European director of the American Jewish Committee] said, . . . two Jews were killed in Meknes last week and one was wounded today in Rabat . . .
>
> In Libya . . . virtually all Jewish shops were burned down by mobs last week, he added, and several Jews were killed. Mr. Schuster said that the police had not interfered and that the fire departments had made no attempts to put out the fires.[50]

This alarming report found confirmation from multiple independent sources. Refugees holding foreign passports confirmed them after arriving in Italy and Cyprus. A correspondent of *The New York Times* wired from Famagusta, Cyprus, confirming that arrests are "terrorizing the 2,600 Jews" in Egypt. He added, symptomatically:

> It was necessary to leave the United Arab Republic to write this article, as it never would have passed the censor.[51]

In Morocco, the mistreatment of Jews has become a

---

[50] *The New York Times,* June 14, 1967.
[51] *Ibid.,* June 15, 1967.

divisive political issue. The religious Istiqlal party was leading so vicious an anti-Jewish campaign that King Hassan II and the government chose to intervene. But then, in protest against this alleged softness on "Zionism," the Moroccan Labor Federation called a nationwide general strike. This in turn led to an 18-month prison sentence for Mahjoub ben Seddick, a popular labor leader.[52]

There were excesses elsewhere. In Tripoli, Libya, six Jews were killed and the Jewish quarter was sacked. In Aden, two Jews were killed as mobs attacked and burned the Jewish quarter and a synagogue. There were also pogroms in Syria, while in Tunisia, President Bourguiba, in a radio and television appearance, issued a warning against assailants of Jews and the government apologized to the Jewish community for attacks by "hooligans."

The Jewish scapegoats in the Arab countries, too, are in a way second-time refugees. Their plight over the two decades since the U.N. adopted the partition plan for Palestine is reflected in the sharp diminution of their community. A mere 15% of the Jews who were in the Arab countries in 1947 remain there. The rest fled in terror, almost all of them leaving behind whatever property they possessed. 467,000 of these people came to Israel and have been constructively absorbed in its society.

But there must be no emotional barter in human

[52] *Ibid.*, June 12 & 15.

suffering. Talk of the plight of the Jews in the Arab countries is least of all intended here to deflect attention from the terrible plight of Arabs. That we have not discussed here the problem of the Arab refugees at great length is least of all a sign of indifference. On the contrary, it rather stems from the assumption that granted Israel's survival, this is the region's most tragic and most urgent problem. We believe, however, that the main obstacle to solving it is political. That is why to stress coexistence in the Middle East is also to work for the first condition necessary for a constructive solution of the Arab refugee problem.

Justified and compelling as is the concern for the Arab refugees, it is nonetheless surprising that many people who explain their interest in the Middle East as purely humanitarian have completely failed to react to the plight of other refugees. It is such phenomena that cause one often to wonder where the line runs between politics and humanitarianism, or indeed whether there is one.

A U.N. Report

Weeks and months after *Grauelpropaganda* had been dinned into people's ears, when no authoritative denial could completely erase the association of Israel with exceptional brutality, came an incontestable denial. On September 15, 1967, Secretary-General U Thant submitted to the Security Council a report based on the information contained in the final report of his Special

Representative in the Middle East, Mr. Nils-Goran Gussing. While the report did not fail to register regrettable actions and policies on the part of all the Middle East belligerents, it greatly vindicated Israel from malicious charges.

Concerning alleged forcible expulsion of Arab population from areas occupied by Israel, Mr. Gussing stated:

> While there were strong indications that the majority of the population had left before the end of the hostilities, reports were conflicting (or, least, not entirely mutually supporting) as regards events after that period.

Specifically, with reference to the West Bank, where most of the conquered Arab population resides, Mr. Thant says:

> During his visit to the area, the Special Representative received no specific reports indicating that persons had been physically forced to cross to the East Bank.

Concerning charges that the Israelis deliberately demolished Arab towns and villages for non-military reasons, Mr. Thant notes:

> Pieces of heavy artillery visible among the ruins, and the detailed description by senior officers of the Israel forces of the route of military advance in the area, left him [Mr. Gussing] reasonably sure that the vast destruction had been caused mainly during the actual fighting and to some extent after the fighting had ended by the military necessity of blowing up structures on the point of collapsing or which possibly still contained unexploded ammunition or mines. . . . To sum up on the question of the destruction or demolition of villages and towns, the Special Representative felt that the localities he observed, including three of the four persistently mentioned in Syrian complaints, did show vast destruction, but that this destruction could largely be attributed to military operations.

Concerning accusations of looting by Israeli soldiers,

> Israel spokesmen informed the Special Representative on several occasions that the Israel authorities had taken measures to prevent looting and to stop it when it occurred, including the court martialling of army personnel caught in the act of looting.

In fact, among the prisoners the Special Representative encountered in Kuneitra were "some Israel soldiers sentenced to imprisonment for looting."

On the other hand, Mr. Thant's representative was met with utter non-cooperation when he attempted to investigate the situation of the Jewish minorities in Syria and the United Arab Republic. Unable therefore to draw final conclusions on their situation, he nonetheless noted:

> The Special Representative indicated that there were persistent allegations that 500 to 600 Jewish men (the Jewish minority in the United Arab Republic is estimated at about 2,500 persons) had been kept in detention since the beginning of the war, and held incommunicado, although allowed to correspond by letter with their families and to receive relief assistance, and moreover that the property of the Jews in Cairo had been confiscated.

It would merely have been an act of human decency and honesty, upon the publication of that report, for retractions and apologies to be issued by all those who had spread so much malicious misinformation about Israeli behavior. While the absence of such fairmindedness is psychologically understandable in the case of the interested Arabs, certainly the Russians and other East Europeans, who never forfeited pretentions to objectivity, and who have not hesitated repeatedly to attribute Nazi-like behavior to the Israeli troops and occupation authorities, should have issued corrections. This they owed not only the Israelis, but also themselves.

Elements of a Solution

M. S. Arnoni

Objectively, all the elements needed for a constructive resolution of the Arab-Israeli conflict are available or potentially available. There certainly is enough land in the Middle East to sustain its entire present population and more if only that land is rendered arable. The geographic location affords important advantages, which are realized only to a small degree. A natural crossroads joining three continents, the Middle East bears today no less a promise of global prominence than it did in ancient times. But unlike in ancient times, the access to seas affords today not only navigational and fishing opportunities, but also unlimited sources of irrigation and energy, in addition to retractable chemical deposits. Desalinization techniques have in recent years made sufficient progress to make application feasible on a grand scale. Even if only a small part of the Middle Eastern stretches that have never been tilled for lack of life-giving water could now be irrigated, a great abundance for the area's population could be produced. The manpower is there with which this can be accomplished. There is also the scientific and technical know-how in the region. All that is needed is a synthesis of all these elements.

But the synthesis depends on human attitudes. That is what makes an already difficult task crucially difficult. If attitudes are to be changed so as to make possible the needed fusion of the available components of Middle Eastern peace and prosperity, every regional and extra-regional party figuring in the present dispute would have to do a great deal of changing. The attitudes of the two big powers, the United States and the Soviet Union, must be first to change. Each will have to agree to stop playing with the Middle East for its own convenience. Each will have to appreciate that attempts at big power domination have become too devastating in fact and dangerous in potential. The Middle East must be exempted from the Cold War.

In practical terms this means that the U.S. Sixth Fleet would have to forfeit its attempts to control the Mediterranean. It also means that both the United States and the Soviet Union would have to put an end to the Middle Eastern arms race. Much as merchants of death are relied on by the U.S. Treasury Department for improving America's balance of payments, and much as the State Department, the Pentagon and the CIA are perpetually prospecting for their proxy boys in the Middle East as elsewhere, none of this can be worthwhile if it also entails risks of global war. The Soviet Union, on the other hand, will have to put a stop to mischievous arming of Middle Eastern countries. There is no reason to doubt Soviet willingness to forfeit arming Arabs, if only the United States will stop treating the Middle East as its private domain.

In addition to the desire to avert crises endangering world peace, there exists a motive, which should cause the USA and the USSR to adopt such a hands-off policy. For if the area is to continue as one of contest and tension, before long matters would unavoidably be further complicated by an intangible but significant Chinese presence.

This warning is least of all intended to echo those working overtime on stigmatizing China as an aggressor. So long, however, as the United States clings to its policy of hostility and provocation *vis-a-vis* China, it is only natural for China to bring to bear such counter-pressure as she can generate. An ostracized nation has an interest in making its persecutors' job costly. This is not aggression; no one would more readily see the counter-pressures discontinued than those who apply them—if only they themselves would be left alone. But given the reality of the present relations between the United States and China, and between the Soviet Union and China, it is predictable indeed that the Middle East, unless it is relieved of its present schisms, will soon show symptoms of yet another extra-regional power's preoccupation, except that this time they will be as worrisome to the Soviet Union as to the United States.

Not only will these two big powers have to abstain from misusing the Middle East for power competition, but they, and others, will have to join in a positive, and expensive, effort to supercede present tensions and conflicts with an imagination-capturing development program. There are, however, dangers inherent even in such constructive undertakings. The needed economic and technical aid is of an entirely different kind than the aid which, since World War II, has been offerd by the big powers as an extension of warfare by other means. A nuclear desalinization plant can be imagined, for instance, not so much as a means of winning desert soil for cultivation but as a bastion of foreign influence and a chain of external dependency. But unless future economic and technical aid is extended by the big powers not as bribes in proxy strategies, but as unmitigated interest in the area's peaceful development, the Middle East's Cold War may only be sharpened.

However expensive the required aid, it would be infinitesimal in relation to the destruction that might be triggered in the Middle East if it is allowed to remain a powder keg. To ensure that the aid would be administered for no ulterior political purposes, it would have to be handled by an international body rather than by any one power directly. In the process, agencies of the United Nations could gain in vitality and international prestige.

All the nations of the Third World should enthusiastically welcome such a new deal for the Middle East. It would provide a prototype of the very world they envisage, and it would bear out a promise that they too may yet have their right guaranteed to withdraw from big power intrigues and equations.

Difficult as it may be to bring about the desirable change in the Soviet and American attitudes, the change the Middle Eastern principals themselves would have to effect must be even more radical. Israel, on her part, would have to make a concentrated effort to induce into cooperation as many of her present critics as possible. This cannot be done without accepting risks, nor without political courage. Israel needs to overcome a disdain for a number of governments, which, however hostile in the past, cannot be dismissed as factors in the Middle East balance. First and foremost Israel must demonstrate an eagerness—strong and determined enough to survive a great deal of unresponsiveness and active dissuasion—for cordial relations with the Soviet Union and the Third World. She must find ways of communicating to those nations that, if only given a chance, she would rather not maintain a one-sided relationship with the United States. While this would require courage to withstand predictable U.S. pressures and threats, in the long run Israel stands to gain immensely more from integrating into the Middle East and the Third World than from one-sided courting of the U.S.

Ultimately, even Israel's relationship with the United States may gain in stability and reliability by adopting a non-exclusive basis. Lastingly, Israel without alternative friends may rate lower with the State Department than a seemingly close rapport now may suggest. Dependent on Western governments, Israel is in for a sobering let-down whenever her interests no longer coincide with theirs. But, an Israel maintaining friendly relations with many powers—Eastern and Western, committed and uncommitted—would present a strategically located factor whose goodwill it might be worth maintaining.

But more than endearing itself to any extra-regional country, Israel must never tire of holding out to the Arab world a promise of mutually advantageous relations. More than anything else she needs to reiterate and amplify her willingness to make a meaningful contribution to solving the problem of Arab refugees. She should shout this from the rooftops, from the United Nations, indeed from every forum available, until it would be difficult to impute to her callous indifference toward these refugees.

The Russians, the Americans, the Israelis, all combined can merely try to induce, persuade and attract the Arabs to the idea that peace with Israel can be extremely beneficial and that it can lead toward a great era in the region's development. But even if the international cooperation required should in fact be completely harmonious and pure—an idyll which it is hard to imagine—the final answer will still be up to the Arabs. On them will depend whether any part of the social day-dreaming for the Middle East will actually become reality. In the final analysis therefore peace and progress in the Middle East depend most on whether or not a truly enlightened leadership will emerge in the Arab world. A *sine qua non* of such leadership must be an immensely greater degree of realism than is yet discernible anywhere in official Arab quarters. What is needed is a new Arab politics, perhaps even the molding of a new Arab mind, so as to bring it into greater rapport with the facts of life. Arab political concepts must be divorced from the now predominant verbal intoxications, from a make-believe world of ghosts, from a mystique of hatred that, roaming the Middle Eastern deserts of the mind, must give way to both mental and actual aqueducts.

The attitudinal change needed is probably too great to be self-induced. That is why nothing constructive and peace-preserving can even begin in the Middle East unless the Arab world is first induced to realize that its claimed prerogative to annihilate Israel is wrong, immoral, intolerable and unachievable. Such realization would be helped along if the present unconditional supporters of the Arabs rendered continued support of them conditional on Arab acquiescence to coexistence with Israel. Any support the Arabs receive without that condition is, in effect if not necessarily in theory, taken as applicable also to the elimination of Israel.

There will be difficult problems and challenges in the Middle East even in the best of possible developments. Even the most constructive course would require time, ingenuity, and coordination—political, economic and other. Even if dreams can be turned into reality, the process is slow and tedious. But none of the difficulties is insurmountable and none more decisive than the Arab attitude.

Rarely in history has a clearer option confronted nations than that which now confronts the Arabs: Construction or Destruction.

When all is said and considered, the final answer is theirs.

Author's Postscript

M. S. Arnoni

I may have, inadvertently, made mistakes in this presentation. My sense of proportion in treating the component factors of the Arab-Israeli conflict may have been faulty. My effort at objectivity may have been inadequate. I may have overlooked factors that should not be overlooked. I may even have, and again by inadvertence, made errors in stating facts. I may have let emotions "carry me away." All this is possible, all this is human. But there is one premise which no amount of disputation can undermine: a just solution of the Middle East conflict must spell out the survival and welfare of all, not the survival of some and welfare for the few. If I find myself in candid sympathy with Israel rather than with the Arab states, this is not because of greater political or cultural rapport with the former, indeed for no reason other than the fact—obvious to me—that Israel's position is immensely closer to the principle of survival and welfare for all than is the Arab position.

My severe criticism of the Arab world stems from no dislike, nor from an indifference to the fate of any part of humanity. It stems from the appreciation that wishful thinking does not alter reality, not even when it is ideological or political wishful thinking. It also stems from the conviction that least of all does one help those in need of self-correction by flattery.

Nor is objectivity shown by one's ability to measure out equal portions of praise, or criticism, where unequal portions are due.

The Arabs should be punished for their many misguided political sentiments no more than the Israelis should for their determination to survive.

But above anything else, the progressive nature of analyses and ideas is not borne out depending on which political group of people or states they suit in theory; it is borne out by respect for life and abhorrence for suffering. Whatever else I may have failed in, I do hope that I have upheld this principle.

Books Cited

Bartley C. Crum, *Behind the Silken Curtain,* Simon and Schuster, New York, 1947.

Jorge Garcia-Granados, *The Birth of Israel, The Drama As I Saw It.* Alfred Knopf, New York, 1948.

James Forrestal, *The Forrestal Diaries.* Viking Press, New York, 1951.

John Gunther, *Inside Asia.* Harper & Bros., New York, 1939.

David Hacohen, *Yoman Burma (Burmese Diary).* Am Oved publ., Tel-Aviv, 1963.

Lukasz Hirszowicz, *The Third Reich and the Arab East.* University of Toronto Press, 1966.

Gamal Abdul Nasser, *Egypt's Liberation, The Philosophy of the Revolution.* Public Affairs Press, Washington.

David Porter, *A Conspiracy of Complicity and Complacency.* Vantage Press, New York, 1966.

Anwar el Sadat, *Revolt on the Nile.* Allan Wingate, London, 1957.

Robert St. John, *The Boss.* McGraw-Hill, New York, 1960.

Joseph B. Schechtman, *The Mufti and the Fuehrer.* Thomas Yoseloff, London, 1965.

George H. Stein, *The Waffen SS, Hitler's Elite Guard at War, 1939-1945.* Cornell University Press, 1966.

Harry S. Truman, *Memoirs.* Doubleday & Co., Garden City, N.Y., 1956.

Index